SAFE HORSE
SAFE RIDER

A Young Rider's Guide
to Responsible Horsekeeping

JESSIE HAAS

STOREY
BOOKS

*The mission of Storey Publishing is to serve our customers
by publishing practical information that encourages personal independence
in harmony with the environment.*

Edited by Amanda R. Haar
Cover design by Meredith Maker
Text design and production by Meredith Maker
Cover photograph by © Jerry Howard, Positive Images
Back cover photographs by (top & middle) © Kendra Bond, (bottom) © June T. Campbell
Photographs by © June T. Campbell
Line drawings by Brigita Furhmann
Indexed by Northwind Editorial Services

Storey books are available for special premium and promotional uses and for customized editions. For further information, please call Storey's Custom Publishing Department at 1-800-793-9396.

Printed in the United States by Versa Press
20 19 18 17 16 15 14 13 12 11 10

Library of Congress Cataloging-in-Publication Data
Haas, Jessie.
Safe horse, safe rider : a young rider's guide to responsible horsekeeping / Jessie Haas.
    p.   cm.
        "A Storey Publishing book."
        Includes bibliographical references (p.   ) and index.
        ISBN 0-88266-700-9 (pb)
        1. Horses — Juvenile literature.   2. Horsemanship{m}Juvenile literature.
        [1. Horses.   2. Horsemanship.]   I. Title.
    SF285.3.H27   1994
    636.1'0888—dc20   94-18484
                                                                              CIP
                                                                              AC

Author's Acknowledgments

The following people gave advice and time to this project, and enriched it immeasurably by their knowledge:
Jan Dawson, President of the American Association of Horsemanship Safety,
who answered more than forty questions.
Laura Gordon, High Brook Horse and Harness • Pat Haas, for fire fighting expertise • Cherry Hill
Howard's Leather & Tack • Steven Major, D.V.M. • Jill Noss • Janet Pucci, the Australian Connection
Cheryl Rivers of River Echo Morgans, whose attentiveness when handling horses has taught me much.
Silver and Leather Tack • Barbara Veith, Bays and Grays Arabians • Judi Whipple, Breckenridge Farm
Thanks to Stan Potratz of the Premier Fencing Company — and also to Stephanie.
Thanks to the Colorado Kiwi Company and to Country Manufacturing.
Pam Adams modeled patiently, countless times, and never seemed cross.

Special thanks to June T. Campbell for her painstaking work on the photographs,
her good humor, and her encouragement.
Thanks to my horses, Josey and Atherton, who have endured so many of the mistakes that taught me about safety.
And thanks to my husband, Michael, who has also been the subject of experimentation.
Thanks to Barbara Kouts, Amanda Haar, Meredith Maker, Gwen Steege,
and many, many thanks to Deborah Krasner, who has changed my life.

Photographer's Acknowledgments:

Pamela Adams, Chesterfield, NH, for her patient cooperation and modeling.
Maude Hickey, Hinsdale, NH, for gracious use of land, and of 32-year-old Junior during many photo shoots.
Deborah Hardy for use of her kids, Gretchen and Stephany; her place; and her horses, Nüken, Smokey,
and Shazam — all on short notice, many times!
Marcia Hines, Hinsdale, NH, for use of her horses Rusty and Cassie, saddles, and trailer (she deserves a medal!).
Joe Plante of Howard's Leather Store, Chesterfield, NH, for giving us full reign of his store to model helmets.
Alan T. Wilson, farrier, Alstead, NH, for allowing me to take farrier shots.
Stoneleigh-Burnham School, John Manning, riding director, and Hope Sheridan, barn manager, who tirelessly
smoothed the way with horses and equipment for a lengthy shoot.
Bays and Grays Arabians, Putney, VT, Barbara Vieth, owner, and Jim Benoit, barn manager,
who allowed me to photograph the facility and horses • Jill Noss, instructor at the Putney School, for last–minute
emergency help with blankets and fences • Meredith Maker

Jessie Haas — for her support and encouragement, and for enjoyable times while on shoots.
Bonnie Butler, Putney, VT, and her sons, Tim and Danny, who were available on a moment's notice
for modeling anywhere — anything! • Beverly Major, for shots of her barn • Christina Brown and her horse Fudge
Jack Pinarak and Patsy McKee, owners of Jack's Horse Farm, Putney, VT,
and their horses Sundance and Taco • Gloria Hooper of Saddle Brook Tack, Ann B. Bowes, and Laura Bently.

CONTENTS

FOREWORD

Why do most horse-related accidents happen to backyard horsemen in recreational situations? It used to be that nearly everyone rode and no one looked upon horsekeeping as a special skill. In fact, in some parts of the country it was as rare to find someone who didn't ride or at least drive horses as it is to find someone who doesn't drive a car today.

So with this great history of horsekeeping behind us, why do we have so many accidents? Very simply, ignorance.

Today, we are three to four generations away from that horse-familiar culture. For the most part, today's young riders don't have parents who are knowledgeable horsemen who can pass down their skills and experience. Even so, we still want horses. If we are very lucky, we live close to a good riding stable with a well-run lesson program and a competent instructor. If we are moderately lucky, we have access to a ranch with some good, gentle horses and a knowledgeable foreman who doesn't think it's funny when we fall off. If we are unlucky, the neighbor has a horse and saddle and says that anyone can ride. If we are *really* unlucky, our folks buy us an untested horse from an unknown source, build a pen in the backyard, and turn us loose with little or no training.

Jessie Haas' *Safe Horse, Safe Rider* provides new and experienced riders in all these working situations and more with the understanding needed to safely manage and survive the horse experience. It is written by a backyard horseperson for other backyard horsepeople. From the nature of horses and their living quarters, to fencing and feed, all the major topics of horsekeeping are covered by someone who understands the challenges faced by the backyard horseman. With this book you will learn how to give your horse a safe place to live, and how to create safe places for horses and people to come together. You will also learn how to develop a cooperative, respectful working relationship with your horse. Most importantly, you'll learn how to find a competent expert to teach you to ride, train, and take care of your horse.

If you read this book and keep it handy, you will cure your own horse ignorance and avoid the most common problems as well as many of the stranger ones. You may still fall or get bucked off — that's part of horse-keeping — but you should avoid senseless injuries, serious or otherwise.

Read this book and learn from Jessie Haas' experience and mistakes. Her mistakes can prevent you from doing the same. We should always try to learn from other's experiences, not just our own bad ones.

A last thought. *Safe Horse, Safe Rider* recommends approved safety helmets. Western horsemen squirm at the thought. At the American Association of Horsemanship Safety, we use the following example. Horses can run up to 35 miles an hour. They lope or canter 15 to 20 miles per hour. The back of a horse is about as high as the roof of a compact car. Would you jump off the roof of a compact car traveling even 10 miles per hour? Certainly not! But, we will all eventually fall off a moving horse. Respect yourself, respect your life. Wear a helmet and encourage others to do the same.

Jan Dawson
President
American Association of Horsemanship Safety

Introduction

HOW TO USE THIS BOOK

When you house, handle, and use a horse, do you know what you're doing? You are handling an animal ten times your size — a fast, strong creature who doesn't speak or understand your language. If you had to deal with a space-alien like this, you'd be very careful.

But since horses are familiar animals, many people forget how powerful they are. And people who aren't familiar with horses simply have no way of predicting what a horse will do.

Sadly, this often leads to trouble. Horse sports are dangerous, with 200 horse-related deaths a year in the United States, and many more injuries to both horse and human. Most of these accidents don't occur during competition. They happen at home, in a casual setting. And most of them are preventable.

To prevent accidents with horses, follow these rules.

- Know horse nature.
- Know *your* horse.
- Provide a sturdy, well-designed, well-maintained home for your horse.
- Stay relaxed and alert around your horse.
- Use sturdy, well-designed tack.
- Always wear a helmet when riding.
- Get good instruction from a well-qualified teacher.

Remember, horses are a lot like cars. They're big, fast, and powerful. You can get into big trouble with either one.

Just as our society accepts the risk of driving cars and reduces the risk by requiring inspection, licensing, and driver education, horsemen accept the risk of handling horses and reduce the risk by being careful about equipment and facilities, and by education. They must think every day about:

- Tack
- The weather
- Traffic patterns

- Hunters
- Footing
- Fences
- Fire extinguishers
- And dozens of other safety factors.

When you first begin to think about all these things, they may seem overwhelming. Your horse seems like an accident just waiting to happen. Can you deal with all this?

The answer is *yes*. People and horses have been living and working together for thousands of years. Lots of mistakes have been made over those years, but most horses and humans survived the relationship intact. You can too.

The most important key to safety in handling horses is your knowledge of a horse's nature. Reading about horses, observing horses, and spending a lot of time with horses will help you here.

Another very important factor to riding safely is your instructor. Horse sports are not a do-it-yourself activity. Everyone needs instruction. The more and better the instruction you get, the more this book will help you.

Your riding teacher will teach you *how* to ride. This book will not. There are many excellent books on riding — some mentioned in the bibliography — that will supplement your lessons. What this book does is give you guidelines for finding a good teacher, the standards you should expect to see set for lesson horses and facilities, and the kinds of things you should expect to learn.

Riding cross–country often takes place without supervision, and there are many safety concerns. Chapter 11, "Riding Out," is one to read thoroughly and often, until the rules are in your bones. Here again, there is no substitute for local instruction to deal with local hazards. From armadillo holes and deep mud to avalanches and ground wasps, each area of the world has its own natural hazards waiting to snare the unwary rider. Know the country, or ride with someone who does.

When you choose a riding mentor, choose someone who's been riding in the area a long time, someone with a sane, long-term attitude, someone with a sound, well-trained, healthy horse. The condition of your mentor's horse is a good clue about the quality of his or her advice.

This book can't tell you everything about handling horses safely. Much of what you need to know you must learn through experience or from others. If you ask, you'll soon learn that horsemen love to give advice. Some is good, and some isn't. It all depends on you, your horse, and your situation.

Whenever you get advice — even the advice in this book — be *sure* to think about it. Your most important goal is to keep your horse relaxed and let her use her mind. Don't choose solutions that rely on scaring, forcing, or hurting her.

Horse sports will never be as safe as sitting at home knitting. But they can be made much safer if you follow the rules, use your head, and keep a sense of humor.

Remember: You are in this sport for the long haul. You want to be riding when you're old. That means that no single competition, goal, or tussle with your horse is so important that you should put yourself or your horse in danger over it. Take your time. Think it out. Get help. Don't be ashamed to give up, get off, or bail out when the going gets rough. In the long run you and your horse will be happier.

Chapter One

UNDERSTANDING YOUR HORSE

IN THIS CHAPTER

Your horse is a herd animal with a basic fear of predators, a need for companionship, and strong preferences for both freedom and a regular routine. Your horse is also an individual with a character of his own.

The single most important thing you can do to keep both you and your horse safe and happy is to try to understand the way he thinks, feels, and perceives the world.

Let's say you don't know any horses personally. You've watched them from afar, you've seen them in movies — maybe you've had a pony ride once. But you've always known you wanted to be closer to horses. Now you're about to get your chance and you realize you really don't know what horses are like.

You'll need to know about horses in two ways. First, what *is* a horse? That is, what characteristics do most horses share?

Next, who is *your* horse? In some ways he's like every other horse. In other ways he's an individual, unlike any other horse on earth.

What Is a Horse?

Horses evolved on the open plains. Originally they were small creatures, the size of a fox. Like all grass-eaters, they were vulnerable to predators, and for that reason early horses were herd animals. They found safety in numbers. In a large group, if one horse didn't notice a predator, another one was sure to. The individual horse was protected by his herd-mates' alertness and by his own readiness to run when they did, without waiting to find out why. He was also protected by the odds; *somebody* was bound to get eaten, but in a large group, chances were good that it would be someone else!

Horses have grown a lot bigger in fifty-eight million years. Modern horses have fewer enemies, and they have evolved powerful hooves and teeth with which to fight them off.

But your horse still thinks of himself as easy pickings for any predator. His internal wiring tells him to be wary of anything new, and when in doubt, to run. To you, this may seem like an overreaction. Sometimes it is, and with proper training your horse can be taught to overcome his instincts at least some of the time. But remember, deep inside, your horse is fearful and always poised for flight.

He's also still a herd animal, with a deeply ingrained instinct to stay close to other horses and to run when they run. You'll see this in the refusal of some horses to leave their herds or companions. You'll feel it as you're swept along in a crowd of other riders; not because *you* want to gallop, but because your horse does. This instinct is one that will always require you to be on alert. Not only must you be alert to your own horse; you must keep an eye on the actions of other horses as well, in order to stay in control.

Your horse is wired to react keenly to the sight of movement. He's on the lookout for dangerous animals, and in the wild, his life would depend on his alertness to very small cues. That's why windy days, when lots of things are in motion, are apt to make him nervous; why he'll stop and look very carefully at your neighbors' dog or sheep; why he'll notice a hundred things out on the trail that you might never see.

But your horse's herd instinct can work *for* you as well. You are the herd leader. Your opinion is valued and trusted by your horse. If you seem relaxed and confident, your horse will tend to take his cue from you.

For more information on riding safely in groups, see page 124.

Habit and Memory

Since your horse is basically timid and fearful, he likes his life to be orderly. He likes the same things to happen the same way and at the same time every day. That way, he knows he's safe.

If something different does happen, he will remember it for a long time. This, too, is a skill his ancestors needed in the wild. They had to remember where the wolf or panther hid, because it might hide there again. So, if something different or especially bad happens to your horse, he will remember the place where it happened or the person who scared him, sometimes for years.

Freedom

Though he's a creature of habit, a horse doesn't much like confinement. In the wild, he would have several square miles of territory to call home. He'd roam all over this territory, getting frequent changes of scenery. Horses *like* to roam, and the modern life of box stalls and neat little paddocks that many horses lead can be very boring. This is why you should give your horse as much freedom and exercise as you possibly can. It will help keep him in a calm, healthy frame of mind.

Fears

Your horse has some basic fears that, again, can be traced to his ancient beginnings as a wild herd animal.

Like anyone else, your horse may be startled by sudden noises or an unexpected touch.

He's likely to fear anything he can't readily identify or that looks like a wolf or a crouching panther. This can be a dog, a garbage can, a log beside the trail, even a canoe on the lawn. The resemblance may seem far-fetched to you, but horses can be very imaginative.

He may fear animals that *smell* like meat-eaters — pigs, coyotes, even humans for example.

He may be afraid of snakes; things that look like snakes, such as garden hoses; things that sound like snakes, such as the hiss of fly spray.

Your horse also tends to fear anything that threatens his mobility. This can include things such as ropes, brambles, or wire that tangle his legs. He may also distrust confinement in any small, dark place, such as a new stall or a horse trailer. Deep mud and water can also be threatening to some horses. As you earn your horse's trust, he will calmly cross brooks and puddles. But his instinct will always be to avoid wet spots. The gleam of sun on water may make him shy. He may also mistake other shiny surfaces, such as plastic, for water.

A horse's fears depend largely on the environment in which he was raised and how much time he has spent in natural surroundings. A horse raised on the range may have very different fears and assumptions from one raised in eastern paddocks.

Common Reactions

When a horse is frightened, his first instinct is to run. That's what has always worked for horses in the wild.

In his modern setting, though, running doesn't work as well. Your horse may crash into fences or other objects. He may crash into you. Or he may carry you along with him, farther and faster than you meant to go and straight into trouble.

If your horse isn't able to run away, he'll try something else. If he's tied, he'll try to pull free. If he's confined in a stall, he may crash against the walls. If he feels cornered and threatened by another horse or by you, he may kick with his hind feet, strike with his front feet, or bite. Or he may crowd into you seeking protection — which hurts just as much.

Your horse is most dangerous — to you and to himself — when he's afraid. When allowed, it's easy for him to run. He doesn't have to think about it. He just puts his brain on automatic pilot and goes. Your job is to use your human brain — which does many things better than a horse's brain can — *before* you get into trouble. You can look ahead and plan how to deal with a scary situation so your horse stays relaxed. When he's relaxed, he can think better. He may notice that the garbage can doesn't really look all that much like a wolf, and that it hasn't yet made a spring at him. And he may notice that you, his friend, are there to protect him.

Remember that your horse is used to being bossed around in a herd by older, more important horses. If you learn his body language and learn to communicate clearly with him, you can control your horse much more easily than you might imagine.

Who Is Your Horse?

Now you know a little about how your horse evolved into the creature he is today. He's a herd animal and his instincts are more suitable to life on the wild plains than to life in modern society.

Still, knowing about horses in general doesn't tell you about an individual horse. In spite of all the general things we can say about horses, every horse on earth is different from every other horse. They're just like snowflakes, or like people. There is no substitute for getting to know your horse as an individual.

Here's a portrait of one individual horse — my Morgan colt, Atherton. He's outgoing and cheerful most of the time. He uses his head in dangerous situations. He won't let the old mare spook him into the fence — he dodges the other way, or stands his ground if he has to. He has a lot of self-control when he needs it.

He's also mischievous, and always looking for what he can get away with. If it's wrong to bite people's hands, how about arms? Legs? Do feet count?

Physically, he's very sensitive, so it's always easy to communicate with him. But his sensitivity makes him dangerous when he's been out in the rain, because it makes him itchy and he looks for someone to rub himself against.

He's more alert than the mare, so even things at a distance can startle him. This makes his jumps harder to anticipate. But because he knows what's scaring him is still far away, he feels safe and doesn't startle violently. When he sees a new object, his impulse is to approach it — yet the sight of my father stacking wood inside the pasture once frightened him so much that he wouldn't even come to his grain.

Many horses resist leaving home and go much faster on the return journey. Not Atherton. He's just discovering the big wide world and he always wants to go farther. When I turn him around to head home he usually balks and stands there looking stubborn for five minutes. He wants to challenge the neighbors' sheep guard dog. He wants to see what's going on at the next farm.

As you can see, this horse is an individual, not a type. You'll get to know your own horse as an individual, too. You'll know what he's reliable about, and what upsets him. You'll know what makes him cross. If one little fly is enough to send him into a tizzy, you'll know what to expect when you see one flying around his ears. You'll know if a punishing spank gets him upset for half an hour, or if it rolls off him like water off a duck. You'll learn if grain is his prime motivator, or if rest and comfort are most important to him.

If you know your horse, you'll prevent misunderstandings. When I first got Atherton I hurt his feelings very much. While he was a foal he'd been taught by a well-meaning person to have his rump scratched. He asked for this treat by backing up toward people. When he backed up toward me, I thought he was going to kick. I scolded him. Only later did I realize what he was asking for. I was sorry, but I didn't mind that he was discouraged from doing this again. The signals were just too confusing!

Getting to Know Him

For information on buying a horse, see page 145.

Let's say your new horse has just stepped off the trailer. He's all yours now. Although you did your best to make sure you got a horse with no health problems or dangerous habits, that is *all* you know about him. Now, how do you get acquainted?

Your best course is simply to spend some time watching him. If you're turning him loose in a pasture or paddock, you'll want to watch extra carefully to be sure he isn't overpowering your fences or otherwise getting into trouble. But even if you're just putting him in a stall, it's still important to watch because you can learn a lot about his basic nature.

Do not attempt to ride a new horse unless he is thoroughly trained and you yourself are a trained and capable rider.

Does he settle down quickly? Does he seem to notice what's going on around him? Has the new situation caused him to ignore people, fences, and food? Does he pay a lot of attention to nearby horses? Or would he rather eat?

All these things are useful clues and can help you tell what your horse is like.

Just remember that this time is very stressful for a horse. You won't get a true reading of his character if you judge him at a time like this. On the other hand, you can get a pretty accurate idea of what he'll be like during other stressful moments, which can be useful later on.

Learning Herd Structure

You should also pay close attention to your horse's behavior in a herd situation. Horses in groups always know which horse is boss. Sometimes it's the oldest horse, or the biggest, but often it's the one who is most aggressive or most active. That horse can boss all the others. The next horse down can boss everyone but the leader, and so on and so on, down to the bottom horse who can't boss anyone.

How does your horse stack up in the herd situation? Is he a bully or a victim, or somewhere in the middle? Does he have a particular enemy? A special buddy? This knowledge will help you every time you walk into that herd. It will keep you from getting in the middle of fights, or from putting your horse in a situation where his enemy can pick on him.

So take the time to learn your herd's structure. Just stand outside the fence and watch for fifteen or twenty minutes every once in a while. Feeding time is especially revealing. This knowledge will benefit you both greatly in the future.

Using Your Knowledge

Most of the time you'll use your knowledge without being aware. But each time you face a new and challenging situation, you should pause to consider how *this* horse is likely to react — not horses in general, and not even your friend's horse, who may be encountering the big truck or crossing the stream just ahead of you, but *this* horse, for whom you are responsible. Taking time to think and having the knowledge on which to base your choices can keep both of you happy, healthy, and safe.

You should always avoid standing among a group of horses during feeding time. For more information on working in groups of horses, see page 57.

Chapter Two

BODY LANGUAGE

IN THIS CHAPTER

To understand what your horse is saying:

✔ Watch her ears.
✔ Watch her body in profile.
✔ Be aware of what she's doing with her tail.
✔ When riding, pay attention to her gait and muscle tone.

Other than the occasional call to you or the greedy nicker with which she greets you at feeding time, most of your horse's communications will be silent. You'll learn to know what she's feeling by observing the changes in her body. This is how horses communicate with each other and, fortunately for us, it's an easy language to learn. In fact, you can learn just by watching!

Watch Both Ends

It's a good idea to wear a helmet at all times when you're working around your horse.

A horse communicates with her head and with her hindquarters. These are the speaking ends, and the dangerous ends. Watch them both when you are on the ground working around your own horse or when you are riding in a group of other horses. Here's a quick look at some of the key signals to be mindful of.

Ears Back

Your horse's ears are her most mobile and expressive feature. As a horseman you will learn to watch them instinctively to see what she is thinking.

Most people believe that when a horse puts her ears back she is expressing anger or aggression. This is true only some of the time. Other times it may indicate that she's listening behind her, that she's afraid, or even that she is a little sleepy.

But when a horse puts her ears back *flat* to her neck and shows the whites of her eyes, she really means it! You will often see horses in groups use this expression with one another. It is a threat, and the threat may be followed up with a bite or sometimes a kick. When you are in a group of horses, afoot or on horseback, be alert to these threatening expressions. Be ready to get out of the way or to correct your horse sharply if she seems about to attack a friend's unsuspecting mount.

Just between horses, this expression doesn't mean anything terrible about your horse's nature. If she pulls this face at you, though, watch out. It is an extreme expression, and you should react with caution. Most horses won't use this expression toward humans; I would strongly advise against buying a horse who does.

Your horse can vary this threatening expression considerably. You'll see it flashed between horses as they pass each other or as one comes too close to another's pile of hay. You may receive a mild version of it yourself if you tighten the girth too rapidly. You'll learn to see the difference between a mildly threatening look and a serious threat. You won't jump out of your skin every time your horse pins back her ears. You will notice the signs of bad temper, though, and increase your watchfulness.

An angry horse will frequently put her ears back and show the whites of her eyes. If you see this type of expression, be careful!

Not Always a Threat

When your horse's ears go back, it doesn't always mean she's angry or threatening. When you are riding or working around her, your horse will tip one or both ears back. This shows that she's paying attention to you. She's listening for your voice or footsteps. This is a good attitude, which increases your coordination together and your safety.

If your horse is bored or half-asleep, her ears will tip back and out to the side at a gentle angle. You'll want to watch for the ears on a sleepy or bored horse to move before you approach, indicating that she's aware of your presence.

If she's frightened by a human or another horse, she will show submission by tilting her ears slightly back, holding them quite stiffly.

In order to be fair to your horse and to understand what she's feeling, you must learn to recognize the differences among all these ways of putting back the ears. You don't want to scold her for aggression when she's only feeling bored, but you do want to be sure to keep her alert. By the same token, you don't want her to take you by surprise when she suddenly attacks a passing pony.

With observation you'll be able to tell the difference easily, just as you can when a human is smiling or sneering.

An attentive horse will often tip one or both ears back to listen for your commands.

Ears Forward

People usually interpret ears pointed forward as an expression of friendliness and good cheer, a safe expression. Often this is true, but there are situations in which your horse's pricked ears are a definite danger signal.

Your horses' ears will always point to where her interest lies; that grain pail in your hand, the horse across the road, the flying piece of newspaper, or the neighbor's yapping terrier.

When you are out riding on an interesting new trail, your horse will usually cruise along with her ears forward. She's taking in the sights and paying more attention to the scenery than to you.

This is no problem if the footing is good and if you aren't demanding a precision performance from her. If the footing is questionable, though, you'll want to regain a little of her attention. Stop and start once or twice, unexpectedly, and wake her up a little. Make sure *you* decide which side of a rock or tree you pass on. She should be aware that you are up there, in control of things.

If your horse is straining her ears forward at a strange horse, she's probably intending to sniff noses with that horse. Loud squeals, kicks, or nips may follow — unsafe for horses and riders both. Be aware of who your horse is pointing her ears at when you're riding in a group, and be prepared to prevent a squabble.

Intensely pricked ears can also mean that your horse is likely to shy. If some new object startles her she may stop, ears pricked and head high, and then leap sideways. These early-warning signs can pass very quickly. She may prick her ears and jump at the same moment.

Still, pricked ears can often warn you in time — and a horse who pricks her ears at every leaf of burdock along the trail may be a horse who is looking for something to shy at. She needs to be watched and corrected — but not too harshly. It's usually just an expression of high spirits.

Another time to watch pricked ears is when you're standing within nipping range. Pricked ears can express mischief, and mischief often means a quick, playful bite.

Fast Ears, Slow Ears

Some horses' ears are constantly in motion. This is sometimes referred to as "hot" or "fast" ears. Others' seem to spend hours in the same position and are referred to as "slow" or "cold." You need to learn your own horses' patterns. A slow horse who suddenly puts her ears back is having an extreme reaction to something, while the same expression in another horse may mean very little. Alert horses move their ears more often, and an alert horse is often a safer horse, since she is less likely to be taken by surprise. A

Upright or forward ears generally indicate an alert horse.

Stiff and tilted ears are a first sign of fear.

For more information on how to handle shying, see *pages 65 and 128.*

very relaxed, quiet horse may barely move her ears at all. Her signals are more subtle and her owner must be very alert to read them.

Facial Expressions

Horses have facial expressions that are subtle and hard to describe. You'll learn to know when the look in your horse's eye means she's feeling sullen or that she's expecting something pleasant.

Narrowed eyes and a tight, pinched mouth often indicate a bad mood. They can also indicate pain — which comes down to the same thing, really. A horse in pain is often cross and dangerous. If you don't notice her problem and work her while she's sick, you could make whatever's wrong with her worse.

But a pinched mouth and nostrils may mean nothing more than that she's bloating; that is, filling her belly with air and holding her breath while you tighten the girth. When she lets the air out the girth will be loose — nice and comfortable for her, dangerous for you. If your horse bloats, learn what her face looks like when she's doing it. And if you spot the tell-tale signs of bloating on her face, fit the girth so that it's barely snug. Then tighten the girth in stages, pausing between each effort to give her time to exhale. You want to make sure that your girth is properly tightened before you mount.

Ears tipped back and out are a sign of boredom.

Whole Body Language

Horses communicate with each other using their whole bodies, so step back, look at the whole picture, and think of your horse's stance as an expression. Watch her playing in the pasture or paddock. You'll see her lift her head and tail just before she starts to run. That's a signal to other horses, or an invitation to play. If you see that expression when you try to catch her, you're probably going to have a hard time doing so.

A pinched mouth and narrow eyes may be a sign your horse is in pain or a bad mood.

Head-shaking can also be a playful expression. Horses often do this while running, and may squeal at the same time. This is a form of showing off and it's fine while she's loose in the pasture. But if she shakes her head and squeals while cantering along with you on her back, expect a little trouble. Unless you're sure you can handle it, you'd best speak to her firmly and slow down to a trot. Be aware also that head-shaking often just means that flies are bothering her.

When your horse is angry or fearful, the hindquarters may seem to sink and her tail may be tucked. If your horse is afraid — maybe a pal is about to bite her — she'll cringe her hindquarters away from the threat. If cornered, she may kick.

For more information on tightening the girth, see page 101.

If she's feeling angry and aggressive, your horse may instead bring her hindquarters *toward* another horse. She is moving forward, but keeping her hindquarters ready for action too. If your horse moves toward *you* in this manner, be prepared to either firmly establish your authority or get out of the way!

Tail switching is another signal that it's time to get out of the way. Horses often switch their tails before kicking. It's part of the language of threat. But the kick can follow the threat very quickly, so be alert.

Look, Listen, and Feel While Riding

Your horse's whole–body language is easiest to observe from the ground. When you're on her back, it's easiest to pay attention to her ears and to the level of her head. After all, they're right up front where you can see them!

Don't forget the other end, though. Horses often swish their tails when annoyed or resisting your authority. You can't see that, but you'll probably be able to hear it.

If your horse is swishing her tail resentfully, review what you are asking her to do and how you are asking. You may be demanding too much. Your signals may be confusing or painful. Always question yourself first. Then, if you're perfectly sure that it's not your fault, ask again. Your horse's resentful mood may pass. Even if it doesn't, you'll be aware of her frame of mind.

Although you can't see your horse as well when riding as you can on foot, you do have much more physical contact with her. You're able to feel whether her body is tense or relaxed. Is she moving forward freely and with a normal rhythm? Or are her steps shortened and bouncy, indicating nervousness or bad intentions? If she's stumbling or moving unevenly, it may indicate lameness. If her neck is high and hard in front of you or if she's sweating more than normal, she's probably nervous.

Your awareness of these things will rarely be this specific. Rather than thinking about each signal separately, you'll learn to take them all together as an instinctive awareness of your horse and your situation. The more time you spend with your horse, the more easily you'll pick up the signals, and the safer and more comfortable you'll both become.

Become familiar with the symptoms of lameness, loose shoes, fatigue, laziness, and illness and be alert for them while riding.

Chapter Three

SAFE PASTURES

A good pasture provides a fairly balanced diet — good horse grasses and seeds — favorite weeds and a way to supplement minerals, vitamins, and salt separately.

To ensure a safe pasture for your horse, be sure to do the following.
- ✔ Clean out junk and farm machinery.
- ✔ Fill in any holes.
- ✔ Remove all poisonous plants.
- ✔ Eliminate rich feed he might gorge on and be mindful of when trees and bushes bear fruit.
- ✔ Keep strangers out of your pasture.
- ✔ Surround your pasture with safe fencing and check it often for wear and weakness.
- ✔ Make sure all your latches and gates are horse-proof.
- ✔ Be aware of how seasonal changes affect the condition of your pasture and do all that is necessary to keep it safe.

Pastures mean freedom to eat, play, and roll in the grass.

The happiest horses spend their days and nights in a pasture. Having a good pasture is the next best thing to being wild. A pasture allows horses to eat often, provides plenty of room for exercise, and adds variety to their daily lives that keeps them happy and relaxed. A happy horse is usually a safer horse to handle.

But putting a horse out to pasture and expecting him to take care of himself amounts to neglect. You must make sure the pasture is safe, you must provide shelter from wind and wet, and you must give your horse daily attention.

Your horse lives there twenty-four hours a day, and he can get into trouble during any one of those hours — including three o'clock in the morning. So be sure that while he's on his own, he's as safe and secure as possible.

The most dangerous things in pastures are man-made junk and fences.

Junk

Do you and your horse live on an old farm? If so, you may be surprised at what you find in overgrown, out-of-the-way corners.

In the old days, country people simply hauled their tin cans, broken bottles, and what-have-you to a distant spot and dumped them. That place may be grown over with weeds now, or covered with many years' worth of autumn leaves. But if you see rusty tin or the shine of glass somewhere, poke around. See what else is there. Some of it could be hazardous to your horse.

Remember, horses are big and fast. Something that may not seem sharp when you brush your finger across it can severely cut a large horse who bumps against it as he gallops by. Horses are heavy. Your horse could bruise or even puncture his hoof on something that would only give you a momentary twinge.

If there's a dumping area in your pasture and you can't clean the whole thing up, build a secure fence around it and check the fence often.

Old Machinery

Another thing you'll commonly find on an old farm is abandoned equipment. Farming has changed a lot in the past seventy-five years. Machines have been invented, used, become old-fashioned, and been abandoned. Often they are left in the distant corners of fields.

Some of these old machines are beautiful, but they can be dangerous to your horse. Look for sharp corners and edges, spikes, rusty bolts that may have fallen off, or places where your horse might catch his foot.

You may think your horse will never go near this rusting monster, but he probably will. In the fall especially, when the grass gets short, your horse will be interested in eating weeds that grow there — weeds he'd never touch in the summer. He may also be curious, or another horse may chase him into the machinery.

If you can't move old machinery, be sure to put a good fence around it.

New Machinery

New machinery can be a problem, too. Machines used to apply chemicals are *very* dangerous to horses. Corn planters contain chemicals that kill weeds and grass. Orchard and garden sprayers hold chemicals that kill insects. These can also kill your horse, or at least make him very sick.

The best thing is to keep your horse well away from all machinery. Horses are always coming up with amazing new ways to hurt themselves. Don't give your horse a chance to experiment with farm machinery!

Visit your pastured horse at least twice a day to check for illness, injury, and lack of water.

Since farmers don't always have enough places to park their equipment, a machine may be left in your horse's pasture. If your horse must share space with farm machinery, have the person responsible for the equipment make sure the chemicals have been drained out and safely stored. *Never* touch farm chemicals yourself. Some of them are extremely poisonous. Check to see that your horse can't get his nose into the chemical tank, even if it's empty. Breathing chemical fumes can also be very dangerous — for humans and animals. Do your best to keep both away from these types of tanks and containers.

Natural Hazards

Although humans and the things they invent are usually a modern horse's biggest problem, the natural world can be hazardous, too. Even things as innocent looking as woodchuck holes and apple trees can spell trouble for your horse.

Holes — whether made by woodchuck, prairie dog, or gopher — should always be filled in. Otherwise, your horse may step in them and injure himself. The best solution to this problem is to catch the pest in a box-type trap and transport it to a new home where it's unlikely to be a nuisance. Or you can invest in a dog who likes to hunt. Even if the dog doesn't catch the pest, its presence will help keep the population down.

Apple trees can pose a hazard, too. If your horse is kept permanently in a pasture that has an apple tree or two, he'll eat the drops as they fall, a few at a time, and his digestive system will adjust. But if you turn him into that pasture just as the apples are ripening and dropping in large numbers, he's sure to eat too many and make himself dangerously sick.

The same problem can occur if your farming practices include turning livestock onto cornfields after the crop has been harvested. Cattle do well under a system like this, but the gleanings in the field are apt to be too rich for your horse. A lush new pasture of clover can also cause colic or founder. Whenever you change your horse from an old, poor pasture to a fresh, rich one, be sure to do it gradually, a few hours at a time to begin with. Also be alert during the spring when many grasses become very rich and in the fall when they dry.

Poisonous Plants

There are many plants, including common ones, that can be dangerous to horses. For example, cherry trees, found around the edge of many pastures, are harmless to horses most of the time. But when the leaves are wilted they contain a powerful poison that can quickly kill a horse. It only takes a few wilted cherry leaves from trimmed or downed branches to cause

Be sure to always make any changes to your horse's feed gradually. Abrupt changes only invite trouble.

HOW TO RECOGNIZE COLIC AND FOUNDER

Colic is the number-one killer of horses. To be prepared when it occurs, you must first know the signs; second, have your vet's phone number handy; and, third, know what your vet would prefer you to do when you suspect colic.

Colic is basically a stomach ache that can turn very dangerous. A horse's digestive system is simple and vulnerable. He has a long intestinal tract that can easily become twisted. In severe cases this can cause death.

Suspect colic if your horse seems dull and unresponsive to you. He may groan and bite his sides or kick his belly. His upper lip may twitch and his gums may turn gray or brick red. As the colic gets worse your horse may roll on the ground.

If you think your horse has colic, call the vet immediately. He or she will want to know your horse's vital signs — heart rate, breathing pattern, etc. So take note of them before you call in. While you wait for the vet, put a halter on your horse and keep him on his feet. Rolling is very dangerous for a colicking horse and you **must** prevent it. Walking him around may help you to keep him up, and can also help your horse pass the gas that may be making him uncomfortable.

Founder is an inflammation of the lining of the hoof. The most common causes of founder include gorging on rich food, chronic overfeeding, or watering while the horse is hot. It is very painful and can cause your horse to become permanently lame.

Typically a foundered horse will be lame in both front feet, and will stand and walk with his weight on his heels. He will be unwilling to move. The surface of the hoof may feel unusually warm to the touch. Sometimes, however, founder produces no heat.

Suspect founder if you see lameness after gorging on rich feed, lameness accompanied by fever, or lameness after work on hard ground, especially if your horse is fat.

Call your vet at once and be ready with your horse's vital signs. There is no time to waste. Get soft footing under your horse, and don't attempt treatment until you understand what your vet wants you to do.

Ask your vet NOW what emergency procedures you should take in case of colic. Procedures will vary from vet to vet depending on the area you live in and the vet's training.

death. It's best to remove any cherry trees that are near your pasture or paddock. Try to do this during the winter when there are no leaves. If you must do it while the leaves are still on, keep your horse confined until you've gathered up *all* the leaves.

Another dangerous tree is the red maple. The leaves of this tree are a beautiful dark red all summer long. They're also highly poisonous and can cause death. The red maple is frequently planted on lawns for ornament, but it's an ornament that a horse farm can do without.

Throughout the country there are many other poisonous plants, varying widely according to climate. Some of them, such as buttercups and milkweed, are common pasture plants that aren't particularly dangerous to your horse. Others, such as yew, locoweed, and poison hemlock, are quite lethal and should be removed.

To learn what plants in your area may pose a risk, visit your county Extension Agent or other agricultural field office. They will be able to provide you with a list of poisonous plants native to your area. If you're still in doubt, ask to have someone from the Extension Service walk your pasture with you and point out any poisonous plants.

Remember: Many ornamental plants, flowers, and flowering bushes are poisonous. Keep your horse out of the family flower bed, not only for the gardener's sake, but for your horse's.

You need to be extra careful about poisonous plants when moving into a new facility or changing your pasture layout. A friend of mine, one of the best horsemen I know, once colicked her entire herd by fencing them in with an ornamental bush that grew on the corner between lawn and pasture. Fortunately, a mild bellyache was the only consequence, but it could have been much worse.

Temporary Grazing

Never stake a horse out the way you might tie a goat. A horse tied on a long rope is almost certain to get tangled up and get a rope burn, which can lead to long-term lameness. If you want to take advantage of a lush stand of unfenced grass, put a temporary electric fence around it. There are a number of small units available designed to be carried along on trail rides. They include a small battery-powered charger. These can also be quite handy for temporary use at home.

For more information on electric fencing, see page 23.

People and Your Pasture

Your horse is dangerous to strangers, and they are a hazard for him. If you have the choice, don't pasture your horse next to public roads. Plant a cornfield, a hedge, or even a fine stand of poison ivy between the public and your horse. Post signs warning people to stay out of your pasture and away from your horses. A good sign that will get the point across without being nasty is, "Don't Feed Fingers to the Horses."

An electric fence will do a good job of keeping people out too, but be sure it is well posted with warning signs. This may be a matter of state law where you live, as electric shock can be hazardous to people with weak hearts. A sign is always a polite warning, and it puts you in a better position if someone does grab hold of your fence and then complains.

If you see strangers, especially small children or adults with small children, approaching your pasture, don't assume they know what they're doing. Get out there and warn them away.

Never take a cat, dog, or small child into the pasture with you, especially when you are entering a group situation. This is a sure recipe for disaster.

The horse's instinct is to chase smaller predators, and that's probably what your cat, dog, or little brother will look like to him. It's not uncommon for pets or small children to be hurt or even killed by horses. Plus, your dog may try to chase your horse, a complication you definitely don't need.

Taking a small child in with horses is particularly dangerous. Horses are often frightened and confused by the sight of small children walking around. They don't look quite human to a horse, and they're apt to make startling sounds or movements.

A case of a three-year-old child being kicked and killed by a horse made national news recently. This kind of tragedy is simple to avoid if you realize that horses are dangerous animals. Keep this in mind at all times, for your own sake and the sake of everyone, two-legged or four-legged, around you.

If there are small children in your household or visiting your family, make sure that they learn proper respect for your horse. Make sure all responsible adults understand that small children are not allowed in the pasture or stable unsupervised.

Fences

IN THIS SECTION

To ensure your fence is safe:
- ✔ Choose a safe, sturdy fencing material.
- ✔ Keep your fences well-maintained.
- ✔ Check fences often, especially during periods of bad weather.

A fence has two important jobs to do. First, it must keep your horse in. Second, it must protect your horse if he runs into it or tries to get out.

Keeping Him In

The pasture or paddock is a controlled area, and you have worked hard to make it safe. The outside world isn't like that. In populated areas your horse can be endangered by traffic if he gets out, and he can endanger drivers. He may kick one of your neighbors, or he may poison himself eating their ornamental shrubs. He can ruin good relations between neighbors for a long time if he eats someone's precious garden!

In rural areas your horse may injure himself if he gets into cornfields or other crops. Grains and corn are rich foods, and if your horse gorges on them he may colic or founder.

For these reasons, you should always be sure your fence is strong, reliable, and in good repair. You need to think about it often, be aware of how changes in weather and season affect it, and walk all around it on a regular basis to be sure it isn't broken.

Keeping Him Safe

Whether you're building a brand new fence or fixing up an old one, you'll want to give a lot of thought to what it's made of *before* you put your horse inside it. Here's a quick look at some of your fencing choices and reasons you may or may not want to choose them.

Board and Rail

A popular fencing choice is the traditional board and rail. It is sturdy and forms a substantial barrier, but has some give to it, which may prevent injury should a horse run into it. But board fences aren't perfect. Horses often chew the rails, which can cause colic. A horse can also kick, catch, and break a leg between the boards. Board fences can also break, leaving long splinters that could injure your horse. Still, a well-maintained board fence is usually safe and reliable.

A well-made board fence

When building a board fence, be sure your boards are nailed to the *inside* of the posts. That way, when your horse leans against the rails he can't pop them off the posts. Also be sure to choose smooth, sturdy boards and check your fence regularly for splinters.

Today there are a number of new materials with which you can build traditional-looking rail fences and avoid the risk of splintering. Two such materials are polymer-coated wood and polyvinyl chloride. Both make safe fences. They are sturdy *and* they discourage chewing.

Welded Wire

There are various types of welded wire that can make safe fences, if chosen with care. The wire "squares" should be small enough so that your horse can't catch his hoof in one if he paws near the fence. For that reason, "no climb" fencing with two-inch squares, or V-mesh fence, is the safest welded-wire choice.

Smooth Wire

A common and relatively safe type of horse fence is a smooth wire fence. The wire consists of two twisted strands, like barbed wire without the barbs. Horses can still get tangled in smooth wire or they can run into it full gallop and be injured, but there are no barbs to cause the terrible cuts and gashes possible with barbed wire. Smooth wire can be electrified for added security.

Electrified tape is more visible to horses. Use tapes to subdivide pastures, as scare wires, and as a temporary boundary fence.

Hi-Tensile Wire

A variation of the smooth wire fence is the hi-tensile. Hi-tensile fencing consists of six or seven strands of smooth wire stretched extremely tight. The tension on each wire is specific and must be checked regularly for proper strength. This style can withstand a lot of pressure and a horse usually bounces right off it. Hi-tensile fence can also be electrified.

Electric

Electric fences have a few inherent risks, but they are also a good choice for horses. They can be made of both ordinary smooth (covered above) or plastic wire.

Plastic wire fencing is good because it is very visible. Available in yellow or orange, it comes in a wide tape form that is readily visible to your horse. You can also get a wide white tape, which is the most visible of all. This means your horse will be less likely to run into it and break out. If he does run into it, he's not likely to get hurt because it's plastic. (If you live near a busy road, you should consider using a stronger fencing material than plastic.)

The other good thing about plastic fencing is that it's easy to handle and repair. It's lightweight and you can fix a break simply by tying a knot. You can create small pastures and change them often to rotate grazing and manage your pasture for good grass growth.

Plastic fence is easy to install with light, push-in fenceposts. Make sure the posts you use are flexible and have no sharp edges, especially on top. That way there will be no bad consequences — other than escape — if a horse runs over one. Be aware, too, that not all plastic fencing is high enough for all horses. A big horse will eventually make an effort to step over it — and succeed.

The "Premier Quikpost" has a cap on top so horses can't spear themselves. This tape is ⅔ white, ⅓ black, which gives it visibility against light or dark backgrounds.

The one real disadvantage to electric fence is that if the electricity goes out, your fence loses its effectiveness. Usually, though, it takes a horse a day or two to figure this out. If you live in a sunny region, you can minimize the chances of losing power to your fence by using a solar fence charger. This makes you independent of the power company, but you still need to test your fence often (see below) and to keep the charger area free of weeds and branches that may block the sun.

One final note: *Never, ever* electrify barbed wire. If your horse gets caught on it, he will be far more seriously injured than on an ordinary barbed wire fence. Also, don't use electrified sheep-fence for horses.

Electric Fence Training. When you first put your horse behind electric fencing, he'll have to learn what it is. This means he must get a shock.

You want your horse to get his first shock from the fence at a moment when he's able to realize what's happening. If he just charges through it, he may get a shock in passing, but it won't teach him much. Besides, then he's broken your fence and you'll have to fix it.

When you first turn him out behind his new electric fence, watch him. If he doesn't put his nose on the fence all by himself, you'll have to tempt him. Put a pail of grain on the other side where he can see it, and then stand back. He'll reach for the grain, and get a shock. This may seem like a dirty trick, but it's an important lesson he'll probably only have to learn once.

A Psychological Barrier. An electric fence is only a psychological barrier. Unless it is made of hi-tensile wire or is surrounded by a sturdy barrier fence, it's probably not strong enough to withstand a horse running into it. Therefore a perimeter fence should never be *just* electric.

In most circumstances your horse won't run right into a fence. But if he becomes frightened or sees his stablemate leaving him, or if you introduce a new horse into the herd, he may start running and forget that the fence is there.

If your fencing system is mostly electric, you should be sure to have a small, sturdy pen with wooden fencing where you can put your horse during stressful times.

Visibility. You can minimize the risk of a horse crashing accidentally through electric wire by making your fence as visible as possible. Choose the wide plastic tape, discussed earlier. Or, tie strips of cloth on the wire, especially in sections of fence that have been used by your horse as a gateway. You can also use this technique with other types of wire fence. It is particularly useful when fencing in a new pasture or turning a new horse into an unfamiliar pasture.

Testing an Electric Fence. Check your electric fence often to see that it is working properly. Your fence charger has a blink-

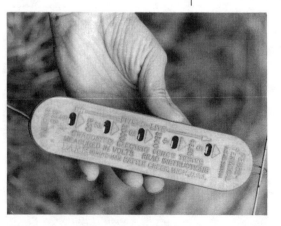

The bulbs on this hand-held fence tester light to show the strength of a fence's charge.

ing light on it, which you can look at quickly to be sure the fence is plugged in. But to be certain the charge is actually getting through the fence, you need to use a fence tester.

This hand-held device, available at fencing supply stores, saves you from having to put your finger on a fence to test it. The tester has a ground-rod that you stick into the dirt and a loop of wire that you touch to the fence-wire. If your fence is working, the tester's lightbulb will turn on. Some testers have a series of lights that will show you how strong a shock your fence is delivering — a nice feature, but not always necessary.

Walking an Electric Fence. If you get no light or your tester shows a weak shock, you need to walk around your fence. Be sure first and foremost to turn your fence off. Next be sure to take along some supplies — extra wire, insulators, and fencing pliers. Chances are you will find your fence choked with weeds, shorted out on a tree limb, or perhaps actually broken.

To prevent your horse from breaking out, you should walk around the fenceline regularly. In the summer months when the weeds are growing rapidly, you should walk it at least once a week. The weeds you broke off today will grow up again. If your horse discovers that the fence isn't working and gets out, you'll have to chase him first, and then you'll *still* have to walk the fence. Preventive maintenance can save your horse from injury, and it can save you a lot of work.

Barbed Wire

Barbed wire is a bad choice for a horse fence. The sharp edges of the barbs can cut your horse severely or even cripple him. The wire itself is so strong that your horse may not be able to break free if he gets tangled, and when it comes loose from a fence post it makes dangerous coils and tangles.

Unfortunately, barbed wire is very common, especially on older farms and for fencing cattle. Even though you wouldn't choose it, you may find yourself with a barbed wire fence anyway. Your first, best option is to tear out the barbed wire and replace it with something safer.

If, for financial or other reasons you must make do with a barbed wire fence, take these precautions. Make sure your fence is in good repair. A loose, sagging barbed wire fence is more dangerous than a tight one. It may make your horse think he can break out, or it may have broken strands that could catch and cut him. Walk all around the fenceline regularly. When you find broken or sagging places, repair them at once. Each strand of wire should be tight and securely attached to a fence post. Pay attention to these details and most horses of average intelligence will manage to avoid hurting themselves.

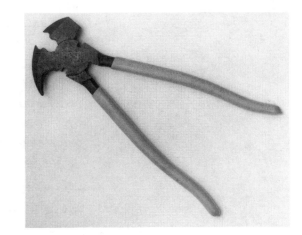

Fencing pliers are versatile. You can hammer staples in, pull them out, grip wire, twist it, and cut it. Hang your pliers where you can find them quickly and keep them oiled.

Some states do not allow the use of barbed wire for fencing horses. Check with your local stable or riding instructor to learn what your state's regulations are.

Next, *put a strand of electric fence* (covered on pages 23-24) *along the inside of the barbed wire.* This is called a scare wire. Placed well to the inside, a scare wire will make your barbed wire fence safer and more effective. Once your horse realizes that the inside wire is electric, he'll stay well away from the fence. If he does touch it, he'll just be shocked and annoyed. This is unpleasant, but much better than being cut or crippled. A scare wire can also be used inside a board fence to keep horses from chewing, leaning, or pushing on the rails.

Height of a Fence

A chain hooked outside the fence is a good way to keep your gate closed and your horse safely inside.

The top rail or wire of your fence should be at least 4 feet high to discourage horses from jumping. If your horse is a sport horse or very tall, your fence may have to go higher. Since horses rarely attempt to jump electric fences, these can usually be set lower.

In northern areas, though, you should remember that snow will change the level of your fence. Snow may swamp and short out your electric fence, and it can bring your horse up to a level where he can simply step out over his fence.

In Vermont, we had several consecutive snowless winters and forgot about this problem. When the next snowy winter hit, a lot of us had horses escape — including me! My colt simply stepped over his fence, which was buried in deep snow, and walked right onto our neighbor's frog pond. Making things worse, he broke through the ice and sank up to his withers in water and mud.

The lesson is, keep your fence high — but not too high. Slightly above your horse's chest level is a good rule of thumb.

Many ponies go *under* fences. If you have a resourceful pony whose method of escape is crawling, you may want to set your fences lower.

Pen and Paddock Fences

This gate is both horse-proof and handy. The pipes drop into sockets in the ground, which hold the bottom of the gate securely.

Pens, paddocks, and barnyards are enclosures smaller than pastures in which your horse is not generally grazing, but is confined for convenience or turned out into for exercise. Since your horse is more closely confined, paddock fences should be stronger than your pasture fence. Paddock fences are more likely to be tested, strongly and persistently, by your horse. Adding a scare wire to the inside of a paddock fence can be a great way to keep "pushy" horses from breaking free.

Boards are a good choice for paddock fencing, especially the newer types, such as coated wood or polymer boards.

The smaller the area, the greater the chance that your horse will hurt himself. Take extra care to make your paddock safe, and keep these points in mind when setting it up:

- There should be no narrow corners where one horse may trap another.
- All waterers and feeders should have smooth edges.
- All gates should close flush to the post.
- There should be no protruding bolts or nails.
- Never fence your horse near a low metal roof or telephone pole guy wires. Horses can and will bump their heads on roof edges or run into guy wires and injure themselves.

Gates, Locks, and Latches

Gates are a weak point in any fencing system. You have to have them, but they break the solid line of your fence. Your horse will quickly learn that the gate is what he goes through to get out. He may spend a lot of time there trying to figure out how to work it for himself.

For that reason, you need to pay special attention to your gate. It should be at least as strong as the rest of the fence, if not stronger. Your gate should be smooth, so a horse pressing against it will not be injured. It should close flush to the post, with no gap between. If there is a gap, your horse will probably try to wedge himself into it and hurt himself in the process. Your gate should have a latch that your horse cannot work himself. There are many different ways to achieve a horse-resistant latch. A chain and hook system works well. You can have a peg on the outside of the gate over which you hook a

A gate made of smooth pipe is a safe choice for an area where horses like to "hang out."

link of chain. You can use a snap to fasten the chain together, or you can even tie it. For all these systems, try to put the chain where a horse standing near the gate can't reach it, or better yet, can't even see it. Another option is to buy a latch with a flange that drops when the latch is fastened (see page 34). Or, get a top-mounted latch system. This, too, is hard for a horse to open and when it is mounted high on a gate, you can open it from horseback.

If you have a gate you feel insecure about — it can be jostled loose, or the latch doesn't seem really horse-proof — you can keep your horse away from it by running a line of electric fence on the inside of the gate. That means you have to open two gates each time you take your horse in and out, but the added security is worth the trouble.

To open this latch, you must pull out the pin and lift the bar, something your horse will find very difficult to do.

Whatever kind of gate and latch you choose, remember: the first level of security is you. Did you latch the gate securely? If you're not sure, it's time to go out and check.

Daily Pasture Care

Good pasture care involves four important practices:
- ✔ Visit your horse twice a day.
- ✔ Make sure he has enough food and water.
- ✔ Provide shelter from wind and wet.
- ✔ Bring your horse in during hunting season.

Your horse can pretty much take care of himself out at pasture, but that doesn't mean you can ignore him. Maybe you don't feel like riding, but you should get out there twice a day and make sure he's OK. Check him for injuries, and watch him walk so you can be sure he isn't lame. If he has injured himself, he has a better chance of full recovery if you catch the problem early.

You'll also need to watch feed levels to be sure your horse isn't getting too much or too little grass.

Keep an eye out for seasonal changes. After all, your field is not the same place in the dead of winter and the heat of summer. Here are some of the seasonal changes to be particularly mindful of.

Spring

Before you turn your horse out in the spring, check to see what damage winter has done to your fence. In areas where the ground freezes, your fence posts may have been heaved out of the ground by frost. Some wooden posts may have rotted. Your wire may have sagged, or tree limbs may have fallen on it. Winter is very hard on fences, particularly in northern areas, and you can't turn your horse out in spring without checking the fences first.

In the spring your horse will need to be confined to the paddock while the pasture grows up. The day you first begin to turn him out to pasture can be a dangerous one. The new grass is very rich, and if he eats too much he may founder or colic. The turn-out *must* be gradual.

Feed him a full, normal breakfast of hay the morning you're going to turn him out. If he normally has grain, skip it today. When he has finished his hay, turn him out for an hour. Since he's already full, he won't be able to

In some areas, spring grasses can green up dangerously almost overnight. Be especially watchful during the first warm weeks of spring.

pack in too much grass. Be sure to bring him back in after an hour, and gradually increase the time he spends on the new grass over the next few days. With most horses, you can reintroduce grain gradually over the next few weeks as the pasture gets eaten down. Ponies, Morgans, Quarter Horses, and other roundly built horses who gain weight rapidly need special care at this time, as they founder easily. The safest bet is to ask your vet for advice *before* turning any horse out.

Summer

In summer you'll need to visit your horse regularly to put on fly spray. If you don't and your horse is bothered by flies, he may spend all his time in the shed or the deep shade, and won't get enough to eat. Or he may get a face injury from flinging his head around shaking off flies.

Know when the blackflies or gnats are starting to appear, and be sure to cover your horse's ears generously with repellent. Blackflies love horses' ears, and can cause a lot of pain and discomfort. When you take hold of your horse's ear to put it into the bridle you'll aggravate the bites, and he may react violently. Try to spare him the pain, and yourself the trouble, by preventing the situation in the first place.

Your horse may also injure his belly kicking at flies, and the injury will attract more flies. Treat injuries at once to avoid infection and fly irritation.

If your horse has a natural water source — a brook or spring — you should check it *daily* to be sure water is still flowing. This is especially important during periods of drought. If you provide water, check it regularly and keep it clean.

In drier regions of the country, flash flooding can occur during the summer months. These quick, powerful floods can injure horses, pull up fencing, and dramatically alter pasture areas. If you live in an area prone to flash floods, check the weather forecast twice daily during critical months. If a flood occurs, be sure to carefully examine your pasture, fencing, and paddock for damage *before* you turn your horse out.

In hot regions, it's a good idea to provide a shelter — two-sided is best — from the sun and wind. Visit it often to check for damage and signs of chewing.

Fall

Fall can be a dry season in many parts of the country. Again, keep an eye on the natural water supply. If you're having water problems now, you'll probably have them through the winter as well.

The greatest source of danger during fall are the hunting seasons, from bird to bear. You should find out exactly when the first season begins and the last one ends. Hunting season calendars are available anywhere hunting

For more information on applying insect repellent see page 82.

For more information on hunting season, see page 120.

licenses are sold or through your local town hall.

If your horse's pasture extends into the woods or outlying areas of your farm, be sure to confine him to an area closer to the house during hunting season. To be safe, bring him in close at least one to two weeks before the season and keep him in one to two weeks after. You can also put a bright halter on your horse, or a bright-colored blanket. Many horses have been injured or killed by hunters, both by accident and on purpose. You should never, ever trail ride during hunting season.

Winter

Winter is the most demanding time for the horse and horsekeeper. Harsh weather conditions will require extra care and attention on your part. Be ready and willing to do everything necessary to keep your horse comfortable and happy during these less-than-ideal weather months.

As in all other seasons, your horse's water supply is of primary concern during winter months. You must check twice a day during freezing weather to be sure it is not frozen over. If your source is natural, you may need to supplement it with buckets of water during freezes.

Be aware, too, of the footing around your horse's watering area. Freezing temperatures and sleet can cause slippery conditions, particularly dangerous if your horse must go downhill to water.

This setup combines the convenience of stalls with the freedom of a pasture and makes a good home for this horse and his pal. They'll both need a few hours of exercise every day to keep them fit and happy.

If your horse must cross ice to get to water or food, put sand or ashes on his path, morning and night if necessary. If he falls he can hurt himself seriously; and if he's afraid of slipping, he may stay away from water too long and become dehydrated. Dehydration is a frequent cause of colic. Don't, however, tempt a horse to cross ice over bodies of water. Later, in warmer weather, he may try to cross and fall in.

Footing is a concern for you, too. Your horse has four legs to stand on. You only have two, and falling down in front of a horse can be dangerous. In icy weather, remember to move cautiously and thoughtfully around your horse.

In areas with heavy snowfall, your fences will "get lower" as the snow rises. You need to be aware of this possibility and check regularly to be sure your fence is still high enough to keep your horse inside.

A pen and open shed is another good combination. Be sure the shed has a broad opening if it is to be shared by more than one horse.

If snow does rise over your fences, you'll have to spend a lot of time and energy making them higher in very uncomfortable weather. If the snow mounts up, it's sometimes easiest and safest to confine your horse to his paddock or stable.

Winter Feeding

Your horse needs more hay in cold weather. If you feel very cold while you're outside, or if the weather forecast is for frigid, below–zero temperatures, throw your horse an extra flake or two of hay. If it's especially cold, blanket him or bring him indoors. If you find your horse shivering, blanket him, call your vet for advice, feed him a hot mash, and warm him with a hair dryer under the blanket, being careful not to touch his flesh with the dryer.

Winter Shelter

Your horse needs access to shelter, either a run-in shed or a sheltered, wooded area out of the wind. It is perfectly possible for horses to live safely and in good health outdoors. That's what nature intended, after all. But a three-sided shelter with strong, well-placed rings and posts for tying and some space for storing grooming tools and feed is healthier for your horse and much more convenient for you.

Your horse's run-in shelter should have three sides and a broad, open front facing south. Make sure the roof is constructed to cast a deep shadow into the shelter during summer so your horse will be comfortable through hot weather and fly season. The interior should be large enough to accommodate *all* the horses comfortably. A broad, open front is a must for shelters to be shared by more than one horse. The opening should be large enough to allow all the horses to escape at once. If you have only one horse, or two who get along well, you can have a narrower doorway — perhaps a door on rollers that can be adjusted in different seasons.

Blankets

Horses kept on pasture year round usually don't need blanketing. They grow a heavy coat that protects them. Occasionally, though, you may want to blanket an older horse or one in poor condition.

The blanket should be designed for turn–out. It should be water*proof* — not water repellent, but water*proof* — and should have leg straps that cross between the hind legs to fasten securely.

If you do blanket your horse, make sure his blanket fits well so it doesn't chafe or slip. Check him at least twice a day, to make sure he hasn't gotten tangled in his blanket.

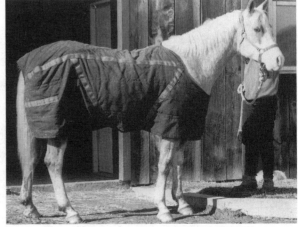

A turn-out blanket is cut freer in the shoulders, and is designed to stay on no matter what your horse does. Turn-out blankets should be waterproof.

31

Chapter Four

SAFE STABLES

IN THIS CHAPTER

Your horse will spend many hours unattended in her stable.
It is essential that this area be well constructed and hazard-free.
- ✔ Choose good materials and design.
- ✔ Pay attention to latches on stalls and feed room.
- ✔ Avoid automatic waterers and electric bucket heaters.
- ✔ Have fire extinguishers handy.
- ✔ Know fire safety rules.

The design and management of your stable is very important to your horse's health and safety, and often to your own as well. If you have the luxury of building a whole new barn to your own specifications, you can avoid many problems. But if, like most of us, you have to make do with what you've got, you can often improve your stable with some minor changes and careful management.

This is a good example of a roomy box stall. Bars on the window keep the horse from breaking the glass, and there's even a toy to prevent boredom.

Stalls

Box stalls are best. Twelve feet by twelve feet and twelve feet by sixteen feet are the most common sizes, and are comfortable for most horses. The walls should be smooth and free of splinters, with no nails or bolts sticking through and no sharp edges. There should be no spaces between the boards in the lower four or five feet of the stall. If your horse rolls, you don't want her to catch her foot in one of these spaces. If there are spaces or rough spots in the walls of your stall, a good solution is to reline the stall with strong ¾" plywood.

Openwork

The upper third of stall walls is often made of openwork material — mesh, pipe, or bars. These can pose a maintenance problem. In an effort to socialize and sometimes to fight with their neighbors, horses with nothing else to do will spend a lot of time chewing this material. For this reason, stalls with solid walls from floor to ceiling may *appear* to be a somewhat safer choice.

The problem, though, is that your horse will end up feeling isolated and lonely. This can make her much harder to handle when you take her out. It's safer for both of you if your horse is in good mental shape. For that reason I prefer a stall with a lot of open work.

But you do need to keep an eye on the openwork and make repairs quickly if your horse breaks or damages something. For example, chewing can leave a spike or splinter sticking out that she will probably slice herself on. Always try to catch problems like this *before* they cause an accident.

Keep in mind that the spaces between mesh or bars should be no bigger than two inches. If they are any larger, your horse may get her teeth caught.

Doors

Your stall door needs to be wide enough for your horse to pass through without bumping herself. Four feet is standard.

Swing In, Swing Out, or Rolling

Doors can swing in or out or they can be mounted on rollers. The roller type is probably the safest, since it means there is never a door sticking out to get in someone's way. This type is also harder for your horse to learn to open by herself. Doors are available with rollers at the bottom and top, as well as with rollers at the top and a track at the bottom. A track prevents your horse from popping the door out if she shoves against it.

If you have regular Dutch doors on hinges, it's safest to hinge them so they open out. Keep your aisle free of clutter — no bales of hay, no coil of hose, no wheelbarrows. Always make sure before you open the stall door that no one else is leading a horse past at the same time. If you take these simple precautions, outward-opening Dutch doors are just as safe as a roller door.

An inward-opening door is *not* safe. You'll always be pushing the edge and corner of the door at your horse. You'll have great difficulty getting into the stall if your horse is leaning against the door trying to get out. If you have a door like this, get a parent, friend, or stable manager to help you change the hinge before you or your horse gets hurt.

Horses enjoy watching what goes on in the stable. The dropped panel here can be raised to close the door entirely if needed.

Stalled horses can become easily bored. A clean old tire, a traffic cone, or a commercial horse toy can provide the amusement and distraction she needs to stay happy and out of trouble.

LATCHING THE DOOR

The ordinary sliding bolt for stall doors is intended to be horse-proof. It must be turned before it will slide. You would think that feature would frustrate most horses. It will stump some, but others will figure it out rather quickly.

You can make a latch like this safer by tying it down in some way. You can pound a large staple into the door, and below the bend in the slide bolt. Then tie the bolt firmly to the staple with twine. Since the bolt must lift before it will slide, this should stop your horse from using it. While quite workable, this set–up can be cumbersome.

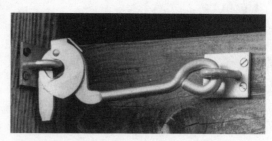

In this reliable latch, the flange drops down as you hook the latch.

Another good solution is a hook with a flange. Or you can use a similar, horse-resistant chain latch. These come in a couple of types, both of which are pretty secure.

Colorado Kiwi Company

If your stall door is not open at the top, it's unlikely that your horse will be able to reach the latch on the outside and open the door. Horses do enjoy hanging their heads over the top of a stall door, though, and if your horse spends a lot of time in her stall, you want to make her as comfortable as possible. You might want to create a spot farther along the stall wall — out of reach of the latch — where your horse can put her head out to socialize without being able to set herself free.

No latch is horse-proof but the Kiwi Gate latch is hard for most animals to figure out. It's also sturdy, quick to use, and won't freeze shut.

Latch for a rolling stall door. Rolling doors are difficult for horses to open and a simple latch like this works well.

Latches

The door latches, as well as the doors themselves, are an important safety component of your stable.

Your stall doors are designed to keep your horse inside. If your horse can open her door, your stall isn't working.

You can prevent your horse from opening her door simply by having two latches, one of which is down near floor level. This isn't quite as simple for you to use as you go in and out, but it beats chasing her down the road or sitting up with her all night after she's binged on grain. Remember, though, in order for the door to work properly you have to close *both* latches *every* time.

Clever Latches

The other way you can keep your horse from opening her own door is to equip it with some kind of baffling latch. There are many types on the market. Remember, though, that horses can be very clever about latches. If your horse spends most of her time in her stall, she won't have a lot else to occupy her mind. Don't assume that an ordinary slidebolt will hold her forever.

When designing a horse–proof locking system, make sure that you can open your stall easily. You must be able to get your horse out quickly in case of emergency.

Windows

A well designed stall will have a window for light and ventilation. If your window has glass in it, it should be covered on the inside with a heavy-duty grill, wire mesh, or sturdy bars set two inches apart. Otherwise your horse may poke her nose through the glass and cut herself severely.

If your windows are open, that is without glass, you want to make sure they are at least chest-high and big enough so that your horse can't get her head caught. You also want to be sure there are no horses roaming around outside the window when the window shutter or door is open.

Lighting

All switches, lightbulbs, and electrical sockets should be located out of your horse's reach. Bulbs in stalls or aisles should have wire cages around them as well. Ideally, all light fixtures in a stable should be explosion-proof. This just means that the lightbulb itself is enclosed inside a heavy glass jar, which will catch the fragments if the bulb bursts. The glass jar itself is enclosed in a wire cage.

Trac lighting is a good alternative to caged bulbs. Trac lighting can be mounted outside a stall and aimed in, eliminating any possibility your horse could injure herself on it while stalled.

All electrical wires should be enclosed in a protective casing, or conduit, to prevent your horse or rodents from chewing them. This is a common cause of barn fires.

Another frequent cause of fires is electrical wire that has become pinched as the building shifts and settles. Examine all your barn wiring. If you have an older barn, the wires may not be in conduit. Make sure that where the wire turns corners and passes joints between two building timbers, there is a generous loop of wire, bent well *away* from the possible point of pinching.

Feeders

Feeders are best located in corners, or higher than your horse's chest level. They should mesh smoothly with the walls of the stall. There should be no

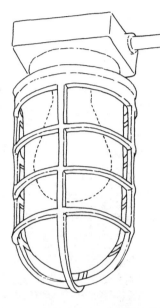

An explosion-proof light fixture. The cage prevents breakage from the outside and the glass jar contains all glass shards should the bulb explode.

These electrical outlets are covered for added safety and the wires run through a protective conduit.

corners sticking out, and, of course, no nails. You can use wall-mounted buckets or tubs — rubber or sturdy plastic only — or feed grain on the ground out of a rubber tub.

You can also buy prefabricated units that mount on the stall wall. These open out into the aisle, so you can fill your horse's feed tub, water bucket, or hay rack without going into her stall. This speeds up feeding and means you don't have to go into the stall with your horse at the moment when she's probably paying the least attention to you.

This hay and grain feeder opens into the aisle, so you don't need to enter a horse's stall at feeding time.

Hay Feeders

For feeding hay you can use the floor, a bag, a net, or a rack.

The easiest and most natural way to feed hay is to put it right on the floor. Be sure to keep your stall clean, so your horse isn't picking up parasite eggs from the manure on the floor. However, if you live in a dry, sandy area or use sand or a dusty material for bedding you may be asking for trouble. Sand colic can be a major problem. You should ask your vet *now* what he or she feels is the appropriate treatment for sand colic.

The next best alternative is a well-made, built–in rack. It should be about the level of your horse's withers, and, of course, should have no sharp corners or protrusions for her to cut herself on.

If you don't have a good rack, the best alternative to the floor is a haybag. It has one hole through which your horse reaches to eat the hay. It hangs by a short strap, so it's easy to hang high enough so that your horse can't catch her foot in it. However, horses have been known to pull haybags off the wall and get the bag stuck on their heads.

If you use a haynet, place its hook high enough so that, when *empty*, the net hangs too high for your horse to catch her foot in it.

A haynet isn't a great choice, because if you hang it high enough to be safe for your horse's legs, it's too high to be safe for her lungs. When your horse eats hay at a level higher than her withers, she gets dust and particles in her nostrils. Breathing these can cause dangerous problems.

The same thing is true of those beautiful, old-fashioned iron hayracks that used to be placed in the upper corners of stalls. Leave the rack there, if

Be sure to worm your horse regularly to keep her system free of parasite eggs.

you love it, but install a new feeder lower down.

No hay system is perfect and choosing the right one depends largely on your horse and her habits, both good and bad.

Waterers

Horses need a lot of water — ten to twelve gallons a day, more in warm regions during summer months. Your barn should have a convenient roll-up hose in the aisle that you can move from stall to stall. Hang your horse's bucket near the door so you can fill it easily. Remember to check, clean, and refill buckets *at least* twice a day and be sure to disinfect at least once a week.

Automatic waterers are a poor choice for several reasons. They can break and flood a stall. People tend to get out of the habit of checking to see if they work. Automatic waterers also make it impossible to monitor your horse's drinking habits. Refusing water is an early warning sign for illness, so you want to know if your horse is drinking less.

Keeping Water from Freezing

In colder climates, keeping your horse's water from getting excessively cold or from freezing can be a problem. Your horse can't drink ice, and cold water *can* cause colic. (Southern horses may be particularly fussy about water temperature, since cold is unusual for them.)

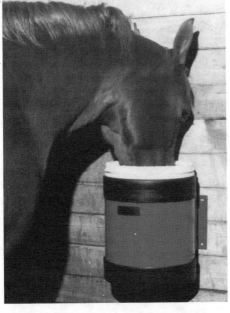

Country Manufacturing

This insulated waterer works like a thermos bottle. Water is kept from freezing without the hazards of bucket heaters.

The safest solution is a product from Country Manufacturing called the Thermo-Bucket. This is an insulated bucket with a surface float on top. The manufacturers claim this device, when filled with cool water straight from the tap, will keep your horse's water from freezing even when the temperature drops to zero degrees for up to twelve hours. This device is completely non-electric and thus eliminates a considerable fire hazard.

You can also buy an electric heater that stands upright in your horse's bucket. Be sure to get a safety heater, with a mechanism that shuts off the heater if the water drops below a certain level.

Your horse must have water available at all times. Lack of water is a common cause of colic.

Hang water buckets securely and near the door where you can easily reach them.

Remember: All electrical equipment in your barn is a potential fire hazard. Do without it if you can; if you can't, buy the safest, best-built heater available.

Bedding

To keep dust down on shavings, mist the surface lightly with water from a hose.

Make *very* sure that your wood bedding products are made of softwood — pine or fir — and not hardwood. Some hardwoods are poisonous to horses, black walnut being the prime example. For this reason, shavings from local lumber mills are not always safe.

Bedding should be non-dusty and free from mold and splinters. Shavings are a good choice, as the content is uniform and the dust is low. They're more comfortable than chips, and they brush off more easily than sawdust.

Your horse's bedding should be deep if the stall floor is made of abrasive material, such as concrete or asphalt. Sand floors should be bedded deeply as well to prevent the colicking that can occur if your horse swallows sand while eating from the floor. Some states require bedding to be at least three inches deep, regardless of floor content.

For a sand, concrete, or asphalt floor, or a slippery wooden one, a rubber stall mat is a good idea. It's comfortable, it keeps dust down, and it makes cleaning easier. Be sure the surface is texturized so the mat isn't slippery. Mats made for purposes other than stalls are *not* an acceptable substitute. This piece of equipment is too important to skimp on. Bite the bullet now on a true stall mat and both you and your horse will be happier in the long run.

Grain Storage

The safest way to store feed is in a separate building.

One of the most common ways horses injure or even kill themselves is by getting out and gorging on grain causing founder or colic.

The horse's digestive system is designed for the continuous absorption of grass or hay, which isn't nearly as rich in nutrients as grain. In nature, there is practically no way for a horse to kill herself by eating too much. She would simply never find the nutrients in a rich enough concentration to be harmful. Thus, the horse has never developed the good sense to stop eating when she's had enough.

We humans, however, have learned to grow natural grasses and grains that are very high in nutrients. Then we concentrate them all in one place, in our cornfields and our grain bins, and we confine our horses right next to these tempting dangers. It's a situation for which nature has not prepared horses.

It is essential not only to keep your horse securely locked in her stall, but also to keep the grain locked away where your horse can't get to it. A latch on her stall door and a locking system on your grain bin or feed room provide a double layer of protection.

Grain Storage Room

It's best to have an enclosed, lockable area in which to store your grain. It must be properly ventilated to prevent mold, dustiness, and spontaneous combustion, which can be a hazard in storing large amounts of feed.

The most important feature of this room is the latch on the door. It should be at least as horse-proof as your stall door. And you should no more consider leaving the latch unfastened than you would consider leaving your horse's stall door wide open.

You should also keep an eye out for leaky roofs, seepage, rodents, and ants. All can ruin your expensive feed.

The Grain Bin

As an extra precaution, have a locking device on your grain storage bin, even when it's locked inside your tack or grain room. If you use garbage cans for grain storage, close and latch the lids every time you use them, or stretch a tight bungee cord across the lid. If you have a wooden grain bin with a lid, install a latch on it, the kind you can put a padlock on. (I wouldn't padlock the grain bin, because I, personally, would lose the key! But you can turn the latch, and frustrate your horse's natural instinct to overeat, which can kill her.)

If your horse is at a public stable where everyone keeps feed for their own animal, it's a good idea to use a variety of locking devices on the bins. A very smart horse can probably pop one lock, but not all of them.

If you don't have a separate, lockable room for grain storage, everything I've said about securing the grain bin applies tenfold. You *must* keep your grain locked up.

If you keep your horse on a farm with other livestock, remember that *all* feeds can be dangerous. Poultry and hog grain often contains chemical and hormone additives. Silage, too, can be attractive to horses, and they must be kept from eating it. If your horse lives with cattle, you must be sure what you feed them cannot harm your horse's digestive system. If in doubt, call your vet.

This grain room is lined with sheet metal to keep rodents out.

🐎 ***Be sure to always make any changes to your horse's feed gradually. Abrupt changes only invite trouble.***

Hay Storage

Hay is a fire hazard and can harm your horse's lungs. You must take extra care to store it properly. Doing so will keep your barn and your horse safer.

When buying hay, be sure to go to a reputable dealer and be sure to specify "horse" hay.

A Separate Space

The best situation is to have a separate building some distance away from your horse barn where you store hay and combustible bedding materials. You can keep a small amount of hay in the stable to make feeding more convenient, but the bulk of this fire hazard should be elsewhere.

You can also store hay outdoors on pallets, covered with tarps. This is less convenient and a little more hazardous. Unless the tarps are well-secured and without holes, some of your hay is apt to get wet and spoil. If your horse eats spoiled or moldy hay, it can kill her. Obviously you should try to avoid this situation.

However, you won't always have the choice to store your hay in a separate area. Older barns were designed to combine many functions, including hay storage. Hay was usually kept on a floor above your horse's stall — precisely the worst place for it, as the dust can filter down continuously. But again, this is a situation many horses have lived with, safely and in good health.

Combustion

The greatest hazard in hay storage is spontaneous combustion. If hay is brought inside before it is properly cured, the fermentation process can

WHAT IS SAFE HORSE HAY?

Hay can be hazardous to your horse's health. Improperly cured or dusty hay can cause an incurable lung disease known as **heaves** — the horse version of emphysema. This can make your horse unfit for work and can shorten her life. Moldy hay can, in some instances, actually kill a horse.

How do you recognize unsafe hay? First, open a bale and look for mold. Mold is most likely to concentrate in the center of the bale. You may see streaks of white flecks or dust, and if your nose is good, you may note a sour or sometimes a mint-like smell. Mold can be spotty within a bale so check carefully and **never feed moldy hay to a horse.**

Next, shake the hay and watch to see how much dust rises. Almost any hay will look a little dusty because it's dry and contains pollen and seeds. But a fine, smoky look to the dust, or an excessive amount, shows that this is hay you shouldn't feed to your horse. Keep opening bales until you find a good one. It should smell sweet and nice. If most of your hay is dusty, you need to buy more. You also need to bring the problem to the attention of the person who cut the hay and ask him to take it back (he can sell it for cow hay).

If your hay is not moldy but seems a little dustier than you like, you can water it. Use the spray attachment on your hose or a garden watering can. Be sure to fluff the sections of hay so the water can reach inside, and feed out the watered hay immediately to avoid further molding.

Avoid any hay that has been treated with mold retardants such as citric acid. This can cause dustiness.

Horses should never be fed from round cattle bales that have been stored in plastic bags. The toxins that build up in this sealed environment can be fatal to horses. (Cows have four "stomachs" and can process most anything.)

Monitoring your horse's hay is one of the most important jobs you have. You must make sure that anyone else who ever feeds your horse understands the importance of good hay.

If you make your own hay, don't bale it too quickly. Be sure it has plenty of time to dry. If you buy hay, find a reliable dealer or farmer. Go to the nearest well-run stable or breeding farm and ask who supplies their hay. Their horses may be ten times more expensive than yours, but your horse is no less deserving of good hay.

cause it to heat up to the point where it may burst into flames.

If you must store hay in your horse's barn, be very careful to bring in only dry, well-cured hay. Stick your hand inside the bale. It should feel cool, or only slightly warm, and it should feel dry. If it's hot and damp, it hasn't cured. You should not accept hay in this condition, especially if you specified "horse hay."

If you suspect a problem with hay heating up — if your barn starts to smell damp or moldy or you're finding a lot of hot bales — get help. The hot bales should be opened up so they will dry. If there are a lot of them, take them outside the barn. Even if they don't burst into flame, bales like this will probably mold or sour, making them unfit to feed to your horse.

Learning to judge hay by look and smell is easy. Ask your instructor, county agent, or an experienced horseman to show you how.

This hook can be used to hang buckets or with a chain to keep your gate closed. The ring above the hook hinders your horse's ability to remove the chain or bucket.

🐎 **For information on safe tying, see page 69.**

Junk Storage

If you have an area where you store hazardous junk — wire, boards with nails, farm chemicals — make absolutely certain your horse can't get into that area. If the area has a door, it should be kept closed and have a secure latch. An open storage area should have a high, strong fence or a working electric fence around it. Check periodically to make sure fences and latches are secure. At the same time, look for tracks or manure, signs that your horse may have visited the hazardous materials area without your knowledge. Be imaginative — your horse will be. And remember, each new horse will think up something others have never tried before.

I once stored a lot of old wire and nail-filled boards in an old pigpen in the corner of my barnyard. The pen had a four-foot fence in most places, and was muddy and overgrown with weeds. No horse would get in there, I thought. No horse ever had in the twenty-four years we'd had horses on that farm.

But one fall day my colt was found standing *inside* the pigpen, eating the weeds. The grazing had gotten poor, those weeds started to look tasty, and he had simply stepped over a low place in the fence to get at them. Needless to say, an electric fence went up the next morning!

Rings, Pegs, and Hooks

A safe stable has an ample number of safe places to tie your horse — rings for cross-tying, good stout posts, well-attached hardware.

If there is a designated grooming area, the supplies should be on shelves high enough out of the way so that your horse can't knock them down with his tail or nose.

There should be pegs for hanging tack. Pegs must be located out of main traffic areas so neither you nor your horse bumps into them.

If you choose to have pronged tack hooks, be sure to buy the kind that has the hooks facing *inward*. This can save your horse from injuring her eyes or head on the hooks. Horses don't stab themselves on tack hooks every day, but it only takes one injury to cost you a big vet bill and your horse a lot of pain. A safe tack hook is a good investment. And no matter what kind it is, hang it out of your horse's reach.

First–Aid Kit

The safe stable also contains a first–aid kit for you and one for your horse. Both of you may need bandaging on an emergency basis. You should consult with your veterinarian about what goes in your kit. Different regions of the country require different materials — snake bite kit, etc. What goes in your kit will also depend on how far you live from your vet, the vet's surgical facility, a hospital, and emergency medical services.

At the very least, your horse's first-aid kit should include:

- Band-aids in a couple of sizes
- Sterile gauze pads in several sizes
- Antiseptic lotion
- Aspirin
- A non-stinging antiseptic scrub
- Ointment for minor wounds
- Antiseptic coagulant powder, to stop bleeding
- Liniment
- Colic instructions — ask your veterinarian for specific procedures to follow and any recommended remedies
- At least three self-sticking bandages, such as Vet-wrap
- A thermometer — get your vet to show you how to use it

Keep your first-aid supplies in a clean, well-organized place.

Your primary first–aid resource is your vet's phone number taped beside the telephone. Don't hesitate to call if you think you need help or if you are puzzled by a symptom your horse is showing. (And always have the number of another vet to call, in case you can't reach the person you normally use.)

One item you may want to have handy is a smooth metal twitch to help you restrain your horse. The twitch clamps around your horse's upper lip and calms her through pressure on acupuncture points. It can make life a lot easier for both of you when your horse is upset and you need to treat her.

Another important thing to have, either in your tackroom or your nearby house, is a good, comprehensive, understandable veterinary manual. Ask your vet to recommend one. A good vet manual can save you a lot of anxiety or tell you when you need to call for help. Don't try to keep a horse without one.

Neatness

Whether you keep your horse at home or board her out at someone else's stable, neatness is a habit you should try to develop. This can do much to help keep your horse safe.

A well-organized grooming area with bridles, saddles, and helmets hung on the wall and a shelf for fly sprays and medicine

If you are the kind of person who keeps your room clean without being reminded, you're in luck. Your natural indoor habits will make your work in the barn come more easily.

But if you leave your hairbrush wherever you finish with it and thread your way through stacks of books and heaps of clothing to get to your bed, then you're going to have to shape up. If you leave your horse's brush in the aisle, one of you is going to step on it and sprain something. If you leave your rake or manure fork around, a more serious injury could result. If you drop your whip in your horse's paddock, she'll probably chew it.

My colt once chewed the top button off my dressage whip. I was terrified he had swallowed it, but before calling the vet in a panic I searched hard and finally found it. It was fortunate that he hadn't swallowed it, since it was basically a large, covered tack. I never would have imagined that a horse could seriously injure himself by chewing a whip, but now I know better.

So if neatness doesn't come naturally to you, *think* about it. Make the extra effort to put things away and keep your stable clean. Don't let old hay or other materials pile up where they could be a fire hazard. Keep all poisonous and flammable materials locked up. Pick up your baling twines so nobody trips on them. And always hang up your forks and shovels.

Slopping Water

Wet floors can be slippery. Don't slop a lot of water around in areas where your horse must walk. Not only could she hurt herself if she slips, but there could be more serious consequences. Horses have a great fear of slipping, falling, and any loss of mobility. A slip could send your horse into a panic or cause her to fear crossing that particular section of floor for months to come. Try to locate your hose and perform all your wet chores — saddle cleaning, washing your horse, soaking her legs, hosing out your trailer — in a place where there is gravel underfoot.

Sharp Objects

Never drop a nail in your stable or paddock without finding it and picking it up. The same thing goes for any other sharp object that your horse might step on. If she *can* step on it she *will* step on it.

Make very sure to impress this rule on everyone who works in your barn, whether it is your parents or a handyman. *Every* nail must be picked up.

Boarding Stables

All of these rules apply doubly in a boarding situation. Depending on the quality of management at your boarding stable, following them may be easier or much more difficult.

A good boarding stable should be well organized, with a place for everything and everything in its place. If it is well staffed and other boarders are considerate, much of this work will be shared. If the staff is overworked and the boarders are careless, you may find many of these rules being broken.

Do your best to get those sharing the facilities to do their part. But if they won't, it's up to *you* to pick up the nail, put the manure fork away, hang the loose baling twines on a hook. If you resent doing all the extra work, look for another place to board. But in the meantime, *do* the work. You're not going to be able to explain to your horse when she's standing there hurting that somebody else should have done the job.

When your horse is in her stall, keep her halter and lead on or near the stall door (and out of her reach!).

Fire Prevention

Fire is the worst hazard of keeping your horse stabled. A horse living at pasture doesn't face this risk. If you keep your horse indoors, you *must* think about it, and take every possible step to minimize the danger.

Have your electric wiring installed and repaired by a professional. Make sure your lightning rods and any aerial antennae are properly grounded. Whatever it takes, do it. It's too important to be lazy or careless about.

In Case of Fire

A barn fire is a very scary and very dangerous situation. It is quite easy to get swept up in a panic, but you absolutely *must* remain calm and think rationally. Taking specific actions with specific goals should help you keep your composure. Memorize the following procedures and be very sure everyone who frequents your stable is familiar with them. A mutual understanding of what to do and in what order will help everyone manage and minimize problems.

A smoke detector is a good investment. Make sure you get one intended for stable use.

A fire extinguisher is essential for your barn. It should be inspected regularly to make sure it's fully charged and you should make sure everyone frequenting your barn knows how to use it.

1. Call the Fire Department

If a fire does break out in your stable, call the fire department immediately. Be sure to tell them where you are and how to get there. Often people call in such a panic that they forget to give this vital information. Try to stay calm.

2. Evacuate

Account for every human being who may be in the barn. Be particularly aware of small children. Try to corral them somewhere that's safe and out of the way, with a responsible person to supervise. Account for every human first, before doing anything else.

3. Put the Fire Out

If the fire is small, try to put it out with a blanket or fire extinguisher. If you know where the fuse box is, throw the circuit-breaker before attempting to fight the fire. If you believe it may be an electrical fire, do *not* use water to try and put it out. If enough people are available, the most experienced person should try to deal with the fire, while others lead the horses out.

4. Lead the Horses Out

After all humans are accounted for and if the danger is not too great, you can try to lead the horses out. If the flames are near enough for the horses to see, you may need to blindfold them, using a shirt or towel. Don't waste a lot of time trying to get a blindfold on a panicked horse, though. It may not really make a difference. Also, some horses will refuse to move if they can't see.

If a horse refuses to move, leave it. Don't risk your life for a horse who can't be saved.

Put the horses in a strong enclosed area as far as possible from the fire and the confusion, or tie them to a stout post. If not restrained, your horse may run back into the burning barn. She may injure herself or the firemen if she's running around loose in a panic.

Keep the driveway and entrance clear for the firefighters.

Smoke and Fumes

Most fatalities in fires are caused by fumes and smoke. You should *never* go back into any part of a burning barn for anything other than a human being. Do not plunge into flames or heavy smoke to save a horse.

If you can see smoke or flames on a large scale, *stay out*. This can be heartbreaking, but it is your only choice. You won't help your horse by dying with her.

THE RULES

1.   No smoking in the barn.   Ever. If you have a busy stable, post signs. Anyone refusing to obey this rule should be escorted off the property and not invited back.

Any stable where you board your horse should have prominently posted No Smoking signs at all entrances. Don't leave your horse anyplace where this is not the clearly established rule.

2.   Buy well-cured hay, and check it frequently in the first few days after it is loaded into your barn. If at all possible, keep hay and bedding in a separate building at a distance from your stable.

3.   All electrical wires should run through conduit. All switches, plugs, and fuse boxes should be out of your horse's reach. Unplug all electrical appliances when they aren't in use. Inspect cords frequently.

4.   Make sure all lighting is out of reach and cover all lightbulbs in stalls and aisles with glass jars to catch exploding glass and stiff wire cages to prevent breakage from accidental bumping.

5.   Avoid using portable heating units — either electrical or kerosene — if at all possible. Misuse of these causes many fires. Obey **to the letter** all instructions on any heating unit you do use. **Never** leave a heater running when you are not right there to watch it.

6.   Have fire extinguishers. Make sure they're the right kind for the kinds of fires you might have. **Never use water to put out an electrical fire.** Be sure to have your extinguishers serviced regularly by your local fire department. Also be sure that you, and everyone who frequents the barn, know how to use it.

7.   Keep your barn free of dust, cobwebs, and chaff. Don't let lightbulbs, fuse boxes, or switches become covered in dust. Clean up all oily rags, remove all unnecessary combustible materials, and make sure all machinery and vehicles are parked at least twelve feet away from your barn.

8.   Be sure all lightning rods, antennas, and wire fences attached to your barn are properly grounded. This is a job for a knowledgeable adult.

9.   Consider installing smoke detectors. You'll need ones especially designed for use in barns. Also think about a sprinkler system.

10. Post the fire department phone number as well as directions to your facility beside all telephones. Know the official name of the road you live on, and try to mark the end of your drive clearly so that it's visible from both directions and at night.

11. Hang a halter and lead rope beside every horse's door. Put it back every time you use it.

Cleanliness helps prevent accidents and fire. Here, each horse's blanket, sheet, halter, and lead hang on the stall door.

Prevention Is Always Best

Leaving your horse in a burning barn in order to save yourself is such a painful choice that if you think about it even for a moment, you'll do everything possible to avoid ever having to make it. That means making sure that everyone else who enters your barn takes just as much care as you do. If they think you're a fussbudget, let them! Your horse's life is worth fussing about.

Chapter Five

APPROACHING AND CATCHING YOUR HORSE

IN THIS CHAPTER

The overall safety of working around your horse can be enhanced by
following these rules:
- ✔ Always speak to your horse as you approach.
- ✔ Approach your horse's shoulder.
- ✔ Move calmly and without undue noise.
- ✔ Talk as you work around your horse.

Whether your horse lives in a stable or a pasture, there are some principles
about approaching and working with him that are absolutely basic. Keep
these in mind at all times and you'll both be happier and safer.

Speak to Your Horse

Always speak to your horse as you approach him and before you touch him.
This is especially important if the horse is eating, sleeping, or daydreaming,
all of which may have prevented him from noticing your arrival. A startled
horse is apt to jump or to kick out instinctively.

Think of this as basic good manners. You have probably been surprised
once or twice by a friend who came up behind you suddenly and touched
your shoulder. The difference between you and your horse is that you didn't
lash out with both feet and kick your friend into next week. To spare your
horse those horrible moments of startlement and to spare yourself possible
injury, just say his name or "whoa," or whistle. Most times you want him to
stand still anyway, so "whoa" is a good habit for both of you to get into.

Remember, then: *Speak as you approach your horse,* and *before* you
touch. If you see an ear move or your horse turns to greet you, all the better.

Approach with Caution

Never approach a horse from the rear if you can possibly help it. Your horse's eyes are placed near the sides of his head, so he can see in a wide ring around himself. He does have two blind spots, though, one directly in front of him and one directly behind him. If you suddenly speak or touch him from behind, you could startle him severely.

Don't take the chance. Approach his shoulder (speaking to him, of course), and make sure he actually notices that you are there.

Take this precaution with every horse, every time you approach. Take special care when approaching a horse you know and trust. Any horse can be startled, and it's the horses we trust the most who are most apt to hurt us, not because they aren't trustworthy, but because we become too careless.

When approaching a strange horse, it's best to approach from his left. Most of the work we do with horses — haltering, bridling, saddling, and leading — is done from the left side. That's where he's most accustomed to seeing a human being. Your own horse should be used to having you work on both sides, but with a horse you don't know, assume that his left side is his safest side.

Go Quietly and Be Patient

Be quiet, and move slowly. Don't be so cautious as to move silently, though. He may think you're sneaking up on him. But you should also never shriek and yell around your horse, and you shouldn't run unless it's a real emergency. In the horse's voice and body language, shrieks and yells mean excitement and the sight of someone running means that he'd better run, too. You could end up with a well-trained horse pulling against his ties, breaking loose from you as you lead him, or otherwise misbehaving.

The running–and–shrieking–and–yelling rule is important when you have friends around, especially if they don't know much about horses. Make sure that friends or family members know the stable rules before they ever set foot on your horse's turf. Make sure they know that your safety, their safety, and your horse's safety are at stake.

Keeping this rule in mind, it should go without saying that you'll *never* play practical jokes around horses or on other riders. If you want to "horse around," go somewhere where there are no horses around!

Talk as You Work

Keep on speaking. As you groom and saddle your horse or otherwise work around him, make sure he's able to keep track of you. Some horses will fall asleep

VOICE COMMANDS

Your voice is one of the most important tools you have for controlling your horse. But not all of your verbal communications are clear to a horse, as not all of his calls and whinnies will be clear to you — especially as a beginner. So how do you know what to say to your horse, and how to say it?

When you're working around your horse, grooming or saddling, speak to him in a normal, conversational tone. Your voice should be loud enough to be heard clearly, but there is no need to shout. Your horse has excellent hearing. On the other hand, don't whisper or murmur. This can be annoying and confusing for your horse, and may even frighten him.

For giving an actual command, a firmer tone of voice is needed. Spend time with a good horse trainer or riding teacher. Become familiar with the way she uses her voice, and imitate her.

Use words sparingly. Say "walk," not, "all right, Babe, let's walk now."

Your inflection matters, too. A crisp "walk on!" means "get going." A low "wa-a-lk" means "slow down, steady." Experiment with this. You can even make a game out of it. Horses are able to understand the tone of your voice more easily than they pick up the meaning of words. Fortunately, we seem to use the same kinds of voice inflections as other mammals: high and sharp tends to be alarming and command attention; low and slow is soothing.

during grooming. Talking can help keep them tuned in. You don't have to babble constantly, but a word as you pass behind him will refocus his attention for a moment on your whereabouts. If you go away for a few minutes — to the tack room for the saddle or back to the house on business of your own — make sure he notices you when you return. That way neither one of you will give the other an unwelcome surprise.

To help your horse keep track of you, turn the barn radio off while you work, especially if you'll be going back and forth a lot. That way your horse will be sure to hear your voice and not confuse it with background sound. It's not a bad idea to get your horse used to radio sounds, so he's not startled when he meets them elsewhere in life. But keep the radio turned off when the two of you should be paying attention to one another.

Applying the "Emergency Brake"

For emergencies, your horse should know two words — "whoa" and "quit." Some people say "no" instead of "quit," but because "no" and "whoa" sound so similar it can be confusing to the horse.

Speak loudly and sharply. Most importantly, believe in your own authority. Believe that you can freeze your horse in his tracks with your voice alone. This is what makes the difference between a loud, unconvincing

If your horse doesn't respond well to the word "whoa," take him to a trainer for a refresher course.

shout and a voice command that drops in front of your horse like an iron bar. You *can* stop your horse. You *can* take command of the situation. Learn this, and believe it. Your horse will hear that belief, and he'll believe too.

Encountering the Unknown

New things can make your horse frightened or suspicious. For example, just because you know all about umbrellas doesn't mean your horse does. My colt kicked at me with both hind feet at his first sight of a synthetic saddle, though he had certainly seen leather saddles before.

Always be aware of the new elements you may be bringing into your horse's life each time you approach him. For some "spooky" horses, even a raincoat can be alarming, or a bright, new winter parka that hisses slightly with your every movement.

If you're carrying something new and unusual, approach with caution in mind. Don't move too slowly though. Some horses will sense your anticipation of a spook and willingly comply. Give him time to get used to the new element, and be aware that he may overreact.

Catching Your Horse

IN THIS SECTION

When attempting to catch and halter your horse, keep these rules in mind:
- ✔ Speak to your horse before you enter his stall.
- ✔ Reward your horse every time he comes when called.
- ✔ Avoid taking grain into a pasture with more than one horse.
- ✔ Avoid being on foot among large groups of horses.

Haltering the Stalled Horse

When you enter a horse's stall, you have one advantage over approaching a pastured horse and one disadvantage. In both cases, that thing is the same: a very small space.

Provided you have friendly relations with the horse you're working with, the advantage to a small space is that you can halter him quickly. Once you've got his halter on, you've established control.

The disadvantage is that the horse may feel frightened and cornered as you enter his personal space. Or he may feel that he needs to defend his

When leading your horse out, keep the stall door all the way open to avoid bumping your horse's hip or shoulder.

territory. He can do you serious harm should he kick, strike, or step on you. In the confines of a stall, it's a lot harder for you to get out of his way.

Fortunately, most stalled horses associate people with food. They are completely dependent on humans for every mouthful, and they know it.

Also, to a stabled horse, being caught and haltered means being taken outside, freedom, and fun. Your worst problem with your stabled horse will probably be that he'll be too eager to get out the door and may push or step on you.

Look into your horse's stall before you enter. You want to know where he is standing in relation to the door. Remember, you want him to turn and face you before you enter. If he's resistant to turning, try to determine if there's a problem before stepping in. Remember to speak as you enter and draw the door closed behind you. Then go directly to your horse's side and put on the halter.

Now you can open the door again. Tell your horse "whoa," and make him stand for a moment — sometimes a long moment — inside his open door. He should come to understand that he doesn't automatically go out every time the door is opened. Your permission is also necessary.

Before you lead him out, open the door as wide as possible so he's less likely to bump himself. You can walk out slightly in front of him, or you can stand outside the stall in the aisle. Tell him, "Walk," and let him come out to you. Walking out one at a time like this is safer as you are less likely to be pushed or stepped on.

Make sure your horse is walking straight ahead as he goes in and out of his stall. If he passes through the doorway at an angle he is apt to bump his hip, which can cause scarring or lameness.

Capturing the Pastured Horse

Catching your horse out at pasture can be a peaceful and pleasant moment, or it can be one of the most difficult times you spend together. Which it is depends on your horse, your circumstances, and how well you control both.

In an ideal situation, your horse will simply come when called — because he loves you, because he loves to be ridden, or because he expects something good to eat. The last is the most likely, and you can foster this expectation by calling him in to feed him grain. Even if your horse doesn't actually need grain from a nutritional standpoint, it's a good idea to use this pleasant experience as a training tool. If he gets called in to a small meal of

Teach your horse to wait a moment before stepping through the stall door.

HALTER TRAINING
FOR
YOUNG HORSES

When you have a young, untrained horse on your place, make sure that he gets good, basic halter training from a well-qualified trainer. This includes an introduction to the whip and to the concept that human beings are not to be stepped on. This training is important for the colt's future life, and it makes him safer to be around during his adolescent years!

grain every day, your voice is going to mean food to him, not work.

Even if you don't want to feed him grain all the time, make sure he gets some kind of treat from a bucket or the ground every time he comes when called. Remember: When your horse is out there a thousand yards from you, you have absolutely no power over him. It's entirely up to him whether he comes or not, so his mental attitude is very important.

Don't be surprised if occasionally your horse doesn't come when called. He may make you come to him — more work for you, but safe enough with the average horse. Remember the rules: Speak as you approach. Wait for him to acknowledge you with either a twitch of the ear or turn of the head. Approach his left shoulder. Put the lead rope over his neck to let him know he's caught, and slip on the halter. Continue to hold the lead under his neck.

Working with the Reluctant Horse

If your horse doesn't come when called or allow you to approach him (or if your horse has broken out of the pasture), you need to handle the situation

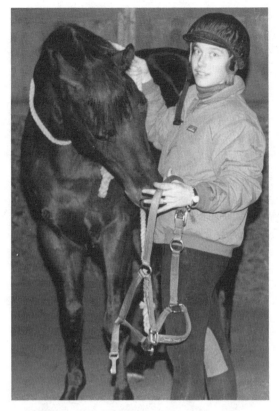

1. *To halter a loose horse, first place the rope around the horse's neck and hold it closed with your right hand.*

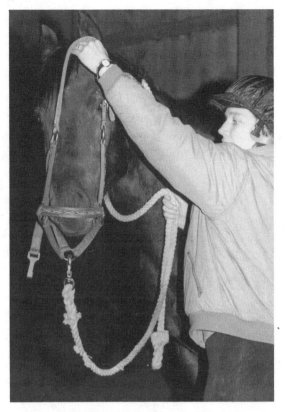

2. *With your left hand, ease the halter up over the horses head, guiding the horse's left ear into the halter.*

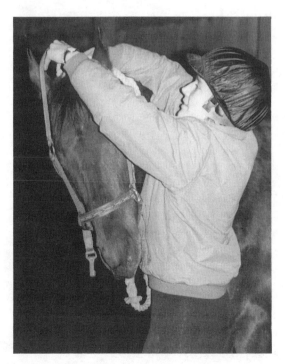

3. *Holding the rope in place with your right hand, reach your left hand over and guide the right ear in.*

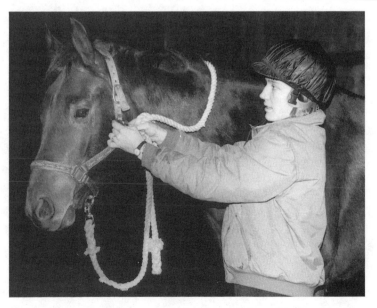

4. *Fasten the throat snap and slowly withdraw the rope from around the horse's neck.*

For more on body language, see page 13.

carefully. A loose horse must be caught promptly, but don't forget that there is some danger involved. A loose horse generally knows that, no matter how firmly you speak, you don't have the power to make him behave. He's more apt to kick out at you now than at any other time, even if he's a very good horse. Until that halter is on his head, he's playing by horse rules, not human rules, and horse rules allow some kicking.

This is a time when it's very important to know your horse's body language. Learn to recognize when he's feeling playful and mischievous. Especially learn to know when he's about to run. He'll usually signal this by lifting his tail. As he runs away he's likely to kick. Unless you're certain you can make a speedy capture, you'd better step back. Do *not* try to grab him. He will undoubtedly win this battle and could easily injure you in the process.

Using Grain as a Lure

The surest way to catch a wary or mischievous horse is with grain.

Walk toward him, call, and hold the pail where he can see it clearly. It helps to shake the grain so it makes that appetizing, rattling sound he knows so well.

You may need to set the grain down and back away from it before your wary steed will approach. Then you must walk up and capture him, making sure to approach his left shoulder. Horses are often defensive of grain, and you should be careful with a horse that has been as hard as this to catch.

When you approach, speak to him, tell him "whoa," and slip the rope around his neck. When you have it looped around his neck, give it a little tug to tell him that he's firmly captured. Then you can put the halter on.

Working with Two Horses

Taking grain into a pasture with two horses can be dangerous. Grain is the best thing there is, and horses will compete fiercely for it.

Always try to catch your horses first without grain. Unless they're very wild or mischievous you can usually catch one, even if it's not the one you want. When you begin to lead that one toward the barn, the other horse will follow.

If one of the horses is young and playful, or if the two often fight, you'll have to take a little more care. As you lead one horse across the pasture, the other horse may come charging around you, showing off, kicking up his heels, or in some cases actually attacking the horse you are leading.

Think this out ahead of time. You will be safest if you catch the boss horse — the older one or the dominant one. Even if that isn't the horse you actually want to ride, the other one will probably follow him to the corral or barn.

When catching a horse in a situation like this, *carry a crop*. Hold it in a very visible manner, so both horses know you have it. And stay alert. As the young hoodlum approaches, speak to him firmly and hold your crop out at arm's length. This establishes a wide personal space for yourself, and the young horse should respect it.

If taking out grain is the only way you can possibly catch these two animals, be sure to put it down in two widely separated piles. Make sure that both horses see you do this. You must do everything possible to avoid a horse fight while you are haltering.

Working with Groups of Horses

Entering a large group of loose horses is one of the most dangerous things a horseman can do. It's like a second grader getting into the middle of a professional football game. You're too small to play, and you don't know the rules. *Don't go on foot among a group of horses unless you are very experienced* and not even then if you can avoid it.

If your horsekeeping setup absolutely requires working among a herd, follow these rules.

First, observe the herd. You will be much safer when you know what to

Use a whip to establish personal space for yourself in a group of horses.

expect from each particular horse. Spend an hour watching outside the fence, at some time when there's a lot of activity going on. Feeding time is good, or when someone else is catching a horse.

As you watch, ask yourself: Who chases whom? Who is dominant? Who is second in command? Who kicks if threatened?

Most herds consist of mares and geldings together, or mares and young stock. Mares tend to dominate geldings. Mares also develop strict hierarchies among themselves, with a clearly established lead mare. If you need to catch one horse and have the whole herd follow, catch this mare. You'll tend to be safest while you're near her.

But be alert. If the head mare feels the need to discipline another horse, she will not pay much attention to the human leading her.

For information on using a whip, see page 65. For information on using your voice, see page 51.

The second rule is, always carry a whip when you enter a group of horses. Make sure all the horses see that you have it. Use your whip to establish a wide area of personal space around yourself. Hold the whip out from your body, where all horses can see it. If a horse approaches, wave your whip and use your voice to demonstrate you're in control.

Stay alert. Horses in groups can start running around in gangs, and they don't always look where they're going. Squabbles on one edge of a group can cause a chain reaction that might end up affecting you, even if you're on the opposite side of the herd. Watch for this, and be ready to take as much control as you can, with your crop and with your voice.

Third, wear your helmet. This can help prevent injury should you get clonked on the head or kicked.

Turning Out

Turning your horse loose can also be a hazardous moment. This is particularly so if your horse spends most of her time in a stall. When you set her free for her few hours of exercise, she's likely to feel an overflow of high spirits. She may kick up her heels, probably not meaning to hurt you, but that won't console you much if she connects. Take some precautions to keep this from happening.

Lead your horse into the paddock and turn her around so she is *facing* the gate. Draw the gate closed behind you, leaving a slight opening so you can slip through. Only when your horse is facing the closed gate should you take off the halter. Then, step back through the gate.

Even a horse who lives at pasture may kick up her heels when released after a ride. It's a good idea to turn your horse to face the gate every time you release her, just to make sure.

You can also condition your horse's response by getting into the habit of giving her a treat every other time you release her. If she expects you to feed her something, she's not going to whirl and kick up her heels when you let her go. She's going to stand there and hope for a goody — a much more quiet and controlled response.

Hand Feeding

Feeding a horse treats from hand is pretty common but can be a big mistake.

The best rule is to hand feed your horse on rare occasions if at all. If you drop a handful of grain into a tub, he'll be just as grateful and a lot less inclined to get pushy or nippy.

There may be times when you'll want to take a horse treat along with you — for instance, when you walk out to catch a horse who is inclined to be difficult. In this case take one treat, give it to your horse in a small bucket or by hand in the correct manner (see below) *after* he has let you approach and halter him, and then make it clear that he is to expect no more goodies. If he is nudging or nipping, say "no" firmly and poke him on the neck or shoulder.

Don't let the warning against hand feeding keep you from giving your horse treats, though. They are a useful tool for keeping your horse happy and willing. Carrots are a big part of many good trainers' routines, and they can be part of yours, too, if you use them wisely and with restraint.

HOW TO HAND FEED

Many riding instructors and associations completely object to hand feeding. It can result in painful, and sometimes serious, nips and bites. If you choose to hand feed, accept the risk and be ready to endure an accidental bite now and then.

To feed your horse by hand, place the treat on your palm. Hold your hand as flat as possible, thumbs and fingers stretched away from your palm. Your horse is apt to accidentally sample your fingers unless you keep them out of his way.

Natural treats are the best: apples or carrots. Very small round apples are not a good choice. They are hard and slippery, and can easily lodge in a horse's throat. It's better to give a larger apple, cut in half for ease of chewing. A handful or wafer of grain is also a good treat.

Sugar and candy aren't good for your horse. Practically speaking, however, one little lump of sugar can't do a thousand–pound animal too much harm, either. One advantage of candy or cough drops over sugar lumps is the crinkly sound the wrapper makes. Once your horse comes to know that sound, a candy wrapper in your pocket can be a very useful tool. You can crinkle it as the vet inserts his needle, or just at the moment you want to snap your horse's picture. You'll have his attention instantly.

Scratching

Scratching your horse's neck or shoulder can also be a good reward or distraction. It may not be quite as powerful as food, but the advantage is that you can always give your horse a scratch. You don't have to plan ahead for it.

But be careful. Horses like to scratch back.

If you have two horses you've probably seen them standing together, scratching each other's shoulders. It's a "buddy system" that works well for horses. When you scratch your horse, his impulse will be to scratch back. This can hurt if he gets carried away and starts using his teeth.

Discourage your horse from scratching you back. Tell him "quit." Take hold of his halter and turn his head away from you as you scratch. He'll soon understand that the buddy system isn't allowed here. If he really wants to scratch back, he can scratch a fence post or a tree.

Scratching Problems at Pasture

A horse can become very demanding about scratching. My colt gets pushy with me out at pasture, bumping me around rather dangerously when he wants to be scratched. The mistake I made was to scratch him in a friendly, social way when he was free. I should have thought ahead and confined scratching to certain controlled situations, such as after work or during grooming. This had not been a problem with other horses, though, so I didn't think of it. It's a good reminder that all horses are different, and what works well with one will be a mistake with another.

It's best to establish definite times when your horse can expect a scratch, using the same rules you do for hand feeding. At other times, a firm "quit" will tell him to get out of your personal space. Don't worry about hurting his feelings. Horses make these kinds of rules among themselves all the time and defend them with threatening bites and kicks. Your words and your hands are quite mild by comparison.

Chapter Six

SAFE LEADING

IN THIS CHAPTER

You will probably spend more time leading your horse than you do riding her. Learn to do it safely.

✔ Lead your horse from her left side.

✔ **Never** coil lead rope or bridle reins around your hand.

✔ Know how to use a whip for communication and discipline.

Leading a horse is *very* different from leading a dog, goat, or even an animal as big as a cow. There is proper equipment to use, clothing to wear, and rules to observe. This may sound like a lot to remember for the purpose of *just* leading your horse. But doing so will ensure that you're both in good shape for riding when the time comes.

Equipment

When you lead your horse, you should use a halter and a lead rope or a bridle. Standing on your horse's left side, you'll hold the rope or the reins with your right hand near your horse's head, below the lead rope snap. Your left hand should be further down, holding the folded slack part of the rope.

What kind of halter you use for leading doesn't matter very much. It should fit the horse comfortably — not so tight that it pinches her head, but snug enough around the nose that it gives you control.

The lead rope should be at least six and a half feet long, so that you have plenty of slack to work with. It should be soft and comfortable in your hands, especially if you decide not to wear gloves while leading.

Don't lead your horse using a halter alone. Without a lead rope you have no leverage, and your horse can easily pull away from you. A lead rope gives you a little more slack to work with, and if you hold it right, it gives you a second chance.

If you're leading with a bridle, bring the reins forward and use them the way you would a lead rope. If something startles your horse and she jumps, you'll have the whole length of the reins to work with. Don't leave them up on the horse's neck. If she starts and the reins are up, they'll almost certainly be pulled out of your hand.

EMERGENCY LEADING — BALING TWINE AND OTHER SOLUTIONS

What if you need to catch a loose horse and lead her at a time when you don't have a halter and lead rope handy? Your horse has suddenly appeared on the front lawn or walking down the road, and you need to get hold of her in a hurry.

If you have baling twine, a belt, or a ribbon handy you can use that. A few rules to remember:

■ Don't tie any rope in a slipknot around your horse's neck. If you have only a short distance to lead her, don't tie any knots at all. Often you'll be able to lead a horse simply by looping a rope, twine, or even your belt around her neck and holding the two ends under her chin.

■ If the horse is more difficult to handle, try to make a loop around her nose, as well as one around her neck. With a loop over the nose you have the same kind of leverage that you would with a halter.

■ It rarely works to catch and lead a horse by the mane, and often it's better not to even try. Letting a horse pull away from you, as she easily can, may make her more inclined to run away the next time you approach. Try offering her a treat, or bring out a bucket of grain. When your horse is loose and putting herself or others in danger, don't hesitate to resort to bribery. The important thing is to catch her quickly and get her back where she belongs.

Proper Leading Technique

Never coil rope or reins around your hand. Your horse could easily drag you and cause serious injury.

When leading, always lead from the side. *Don't* walk directly in front of your horse with the rope slackly connecting the two of you. For one thing, you don't have eyes in the back of your head, so you won't know what your horse is doing. She may be frightened, mischievous, or in a bad mood, all of which could spell trouble.

For another thing, if your horse is startled and jumps forward, or if she decides she's in more of a hurry than you are, you'll be right in her path. You could be caught by surprise and trampled. It's a simple rule and easy to follow: never get in front of your horse's front feet.

Instead, walk *beside* her. Most horses are taught to be led from their left side. That means you stand beside *her left* side, just forward of her shoulder, with the rope in your *right* hand. Hold your hand level with the halter ring. Between the ring and your hand leave a short amount of slack rope. That slack should remain at all times unless you're actually steering or stopping your horse.

Fold the rest of the lead rope so there isn't a lot flopping around. Hold the folded rope in your left hand. This gives you a second chance, should your horse jump suddenly and cause you to lose hold with your right hand.

Never wrap any part of the lead rope around either hand or around any part of your body. And *don't* coil your rope. Fold it in flat loops. A folded rope won't tighten around your hand or fingers if your horse pulls. In general, you want to remain firmly connected to your horse. But situations may arise when your safety may depend on being able to let go quickly. If the rope is wrapped around your hand, you could be dragged.

If you are carrying a whip, hold it in your left hand as well. This may feel like an awkward bundle at first, but you'll soon learn how to manage it.

Always lead from your horse's left. Be sure to keep the rope slack unless you are giving your horse a command.

Stepping Out

When leading your horse, use both voice commands and body signals to tell her what to do. Say "walk on," and at the same time step forward so that you are level with her head. Many people lead from a position farther back near the horse's shoulder, and you may have been taught to do it this way. But unless you are unusually tall or are leading a Shetland pony, this puts you in a position where you can't see anything off to the right of your horse. If there's something over there to shy at or an obstacle to be avoided, you won't know about it until it's too late. If your horse should shy at something off to the right, you'll not only be surprised, you'll also be bumped or, worse yet, trampled.

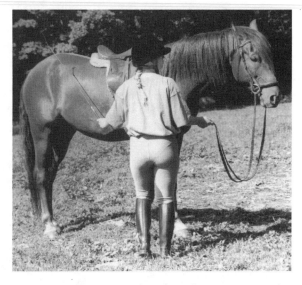

To get your horse used to the whip, run it gently over both sides of her body. Don't tickle!

So get up level with her head. You can keep track of her emotions better that way too, and she can more easily see you.

Any horse you have bought using the guidelines in this book (see page 145) should be trained to lead easily. She'll step out when you do or when you say "walk on." She'll respect your personal space. She won't try to crowd or cling or step all over you.

If she does tend to get too close — and many horses do — you should carry a whip. You can use it to poke her in the neck or shoulder and push her away from you. Tell her "quit" every time she gets too close, and give her a poke or a light swat. She should learn her proper position quickly.

When turning, turn your horse *away* from you. You will be walking around the *outside* of the turn. This gives you more control over your horse. (Horses turn each other this way, so it is instinctive and understood.)

Stopping

When you want to stop, tell your horse "whoa." At the same time you can turn slightly toward her and hold your whip — still in your left hand — in front of her like a closed gate. This gives her a visual signal and helps reinforce your command. You shouldn't have to pull on your horse's halter to start or stop her. If you do, she needs further training. At most a light, quick tug when starting to walk, and perhaps another one when stopping, will do the trick.

A whip can help you communicate. Close the crop in front of your horse like a gate and say "whoa."

Note especially the word *quick.* As you know, your horse is much stronger than you, and you can't literally force her to do anything. Your pressure on the halter should be an act of communication rather than force. It's a signal; then you slacken off, and give her a chance to respond. Hanging on tight to her head and not releasing the pressure is like a conversation where you never let the other person say a word. Sooner or later she either starts to ignore you, or she gets annoyed. So remember that slack between your hand and her head, and get it back again as quickly as possible after every signal.

Bolting

If your horse bolts straight ahead or is plowing along ignoring you, it can be difficult to stop her. Pulling straight backward on the halter just doesn't have much physical effect on a horse.

To give yourself an advantage, step away from her and pull out to the side. This gives you much better leverage, as you are pulling on the side of her head. She should snap right around to face you. You've regained her attention, and you now have the chance to regain control.

Shying

Let's assume you're leading your horse through your own front yard and everything looks quite familiar and ordinary to you. But your horse hasn't been out in the front yard in two days. In the meantime your father has left his canoe on the lawn. The picnic umbrella has been put up. A tarp has been spread over the woodpile.

How scared is your horse likely to be? Each horse will react differently, and it is your business to know if your horse is a sudden leaper, a balker, or simply the kind who rolls her eyes and snorts a little. For the sake of safety, though, it's best to assume that anything new, particularly if it's flapping noisily or even remotely resembles a crouching predator, will startle your horse.

The first thing to do is take a good firm grip on the rope. This doesn't mean putting any additional pressure on your horse's halter yet — that isn't warranted unless she shies. Besides, you may signal that you're expecting her to misbehave. Many horses, given a signal like this, are only too happy to oblige!

Next, think about the situation. Can your horse see the object yet? Which way can you approach so that she sees the canoe or umbrella from a little distance? You don't want her to be right on top of it before she knows it's there. Her surprise — and her leap — will be much more violent in that case.

If the new object *does* frighten her, which way is she going to jump? You want to arrange things so she doesn't land on top of you. In general, try to walk *between* your horse and the object that is likely to frighten her. That way she'll jump *away* from you. You won't be trampled or bumped and will therefore be much more likely to stay in control.

Also, your willingness to go near the terrifying canoe or picnic umbrella may give your horse confidence. In situations like this she will regard you as the herd leader, and as such, your opinion carries a lot of weight.

Give Slack

If she does shy, give her a little slack. That's why you have both hands on the lead rope. Let go with the hand nearest her head, and grab on again farther down the rope. Hold your elbows close to your sides and make your arms rigid, so she can't yank them out of the sockets. Be prepared to take a step or two (or three or four) with your horse. If you try to keep your feet firmly rooted in one spot, your horse may pull you over.

You give your horse slack for two reasons. One, you really *can't* hold her if she jumps, so you may as well not even try. Two, if you try to hold a horse tightly in a frightening situation, she may feel claustrophobic. To her way of thinking, her safety and well-being depend on her ability to flee. If you make her feel too tightly controlled, you may make the situation worse.

After the Shy

If you handle her right, your shying horse will only jump once. Then she'll come up against your stiff arms. You'll tell her "whoa", and you'll speak to her calmly and firmly. She should stand now, more or less steadily. If she's really frightened, she may do a lot of snorting. She'll bob her head up and down, trying to bring the strange object into focus. (If she was just fooling around with you, she may drop her head at this point and start eating the lawn!)

In either case, the next step is to let her see and smell the strange object. Lead her up to it slowly, letting her pause if she wants to. It's important to let her smell any stationary object that has frightened her — within reason, of course. If she's still jumping out of her skin about it, you may choose to do this work over the course of a few days.

Often when a horse actually gets close enough to smell the picnic umbrella or the canoe and touch it with her nose, she will seem to relax completely. She'll give a big sigh, she may even bite or lick the object, or she may try to graze on the lawn. This is great — but do take her around to the *other* side of the object. Come up to it from a different direction. And be prepared, as you turn her and lead her *away* from the object, to have her jump again as if she's just discovered it. Because of the way her eyes are set in her head and the way her brain interprets visual signals, what your horse has seen out of one eye may seem completely unfamiliar when she sees it with the other. Some horses don't have as much trouble with this as others, but in any case, always expect a reaction. Then you won't be unpleasantly surprised.

The Next Time

Just because your horse has walked up to an object once, don't expect her to be fearless the next time she sees it. Her reaction may not be as extreme, but you should still be prepared the next time you pass. Try not to signal your expectations to her, though. If her reaction to a harmless object doesn't diminish considerably in a few days, she's probably pulling your leg. There comes a time when a smack and a stern word become necessary.

Your Clothing

What you wear while leading is as important to your safety as the equipment you use. Just because you're leading a small distance is no excuse for being lazy about a helmet, gloves, or footwear. The pain you experience from an accident will be the same no matter how far you lead.

Helmets

Most safety organizations now recommend wearing a helmet at all times while handling a horse. Non-mounted horse accidents are common, and a helmet can make some accidents less serious. It's very common to have a horse bump your head with hers, which can be very painful. Kicks to the head can be fatal. Modern helmets are cool and comfortable, and wearing one at all times is a *very good* idea.

Footwear

There is almost nothing more painful than having your horse step on your bare foot. She'll stand there forever, while you gasp and shove at her, and as she moves off she'll give you a final bruising grind. It's unlikely she means you any harm, but that knowledge won't bring any relief to your aching foot.

To protect against this, *wear sturdy shoes or boots at all times when handling your horse.* Not bare feet, not sandals, and not light canvas

---

A WORD ABOUT TETANUS

Tetanus is a serious, often fatal disease caused by the bacteria *Clostridium tetani,* which enters the body through wounds. It causes muscle seizures and paralysis.

Horses carry the *Clostridium tetani* bacteria. Your horse should be vaccinated against tetanus, and so should you. Find out if you have had a tetanus shot recently, and if not, get a booster shot. If you should be cut by your horse, stepped on and punctured by a horseshoe nail, or if you stab yourself with your manure fork, get another booster shot. It could save your life.

In the meantime, choose good solid–soled shoes and *wear them!* This will prevent most small puncture wounds — the most dangerous kind — and will keep wounds from contact with manure or manure-dust.

For more information on helmets and boots, see pages 84 and 88.

sneakers, but *solid* paddock boots, riding boots, or work or barn boots. Shoes or boots offer some protection against the sheer weight and crushing power of your horse's feet. Leather boots are especially good because your horse's foot may slide off them, lessening the damage. Rubber and imitation leather are also good choices. Apart from helping you avoid a nasty bruise or broken bone, good shoes also protect you from tetanus. (See page 67).

Gloves

It's a good idea to wear gloves when leading your horse. They'll give you a better grip, and if your horse pulls back they'll protect your hands from a nasty rope burn. Make sure your gloves fit, though. An oversized pair of your parent's gloves are worse than no gloves at all. Proper fitting gloves should be snug, but not too tight, and you should be able to move your fingers freely. Ask at your local tack shop to try on several pairs of riding gloves and for tips on fit.

Chapter Seven

SAFE TYING

IN THIS CHAPTER

Safe tying ensures the comfort and safety of your horse. Take the time
to do it right.
- ✔ Only tie your horse to a sturdy post or ring.
- ✔ Tie him with a quick-release knot or snap.
- ✔ Tie him high and short.
- ✔ Never leave a horse alone on cross-ties.

Let's assume you've safely led your horse from his stall or pasture and now
you're going to groom him. What is the safe way to tie him? Here are a few
rules to follow that will help keep both of you safe.

Safe Tying Rules

Remember, tying is a form of restraint, and restraint and horses don't always
mix. You need to be able to tie your horse, and you should never buy a
horse who will not stand patiently when tied. But the unexpected can and
will happen. Even a perfectly trained horse will someday pull against the
rope. When he does, you want the consequences to be slight. The following
five simple guidelines will help ensure this.

Rule #1.
   Only tie a horse to something that can't be moved or broken. This
may sound obvious, but think about it carefully. You may not be able to tear
a board off the paddock fence with your bare hands, but your horse can rip
it off — no sweat. I once saw an average-sized mare move the large manure
spreader she was tied to several feet. The clacking of the gears caused the
mare severe alarm. I certainly would never have dreamed she could have
budged it.

I once tied my own mare to a very heavy gate and left her for a few minutes. When I returned, gate and horse were gone. She had pulled the gate off its hinges and dragged it into her lean-to shelter, where she was trapped with the gate on top of her.

There is *no end* to the damage an improperly tied horse can cause. In both these instances we were very lucky. No injury resulted, to horses or humans. But it could easily have turned out otherwise. So think very hard, and prepare well, before you tie your horse to anything.

Rule #2.

Do not tie your horse to any part of a wire fence. (That includes the post!) Just imagine what could happen if your horse pawed the wire or pulled and broke that seemingly sturdy fence post. You could be spending the next six months doctoring this horse, and that's if both of you are lucky.

Rule #3.

Never tie your horse using any kind of rope around his neck. As with many of these unbreakable rules, I have broken this one. I once put an old, rotten piece of baling twine around my mare's neck and tied her. I did it because I was in a hurry, because I didn't want to run and get her halter, and because it was "just for a second." I had the very unpleasant experience of seeing her nearly strangle herself before she broke the twine. This one bears repeating: *Never tie your horse using a rope around his neck.*

Rule #4.

Tie your horse so you can release him quickly and safely if you need to. There are several ways to do this. If you're using cross-ties you should be sure they have panic snaps. You can also get single ties with panic snaps. These work very well, even if your horse is pulling back and putting heavy pressure on them.

The other way to be sure you can release your horse is to use a quick-release knot, described on the next page.

Rule #5.

Carry a sharp pocketknife with you at all times. Despite all your care, unexpected situations will arise. You may someday find yourself needing to cut your horse free — from a rope, a harness strap, or an entanglement in his turnout blanket. There is nothing worse than not having that knife when you need it, so get in the habit of carrying it always. And *never tie your horse with anything that can't be cut.*

Panic snaps, open and closed

QUICK–RELEASE KNOTS

Whether you're tying your horse to a single post or cross-tying, you can use a quick-release knot. I recommend the following version of the quick-release as it seems to work much better than the classic slip knot I originally learned. The earlier version — I learned it in 4-H, so it was called the 4-H knot — is quick-release only if there is **no** emergency. When a horse pulls against it, it tightens up. You **can** still release it, if you're very strong, but it's not reliable. This new knot will release even when a horse is pulling strongly.

Practice this knot without a horse attached until you've mastered it.

1. Fold the rope to make a loop about 8 inches long and leaving about 6 inches of the end free.

2. Pass the loop through the tie ring.

3. Now twist the rope several times, leaving a small bit of open loop at the end.

4. Pass a short loop of the section of the rope that leads back to your horse through the loop. (The thicker section of rope in this photo is the horse-end.)

*5. Now pass a short loop of the **end section** through the second (horse-end) loop, pull on the horse-end of the rope, and draw the whole knot snug.*

To release this knot, simply pull the free end of the rope. The whole knot will come undone and the rope will be entirely free of the ring in an instant. When other slip knots come free, they still leave the rope passing through the tie ring. Your horse isn't entirely free, and you have to shift your hands on the rope in order to avoid being pulled through the ring as well.

This quick-release knot works well with round ropes, but is less successful with flat web lead shanks. For best results, use a round cotton or nylon rope.

As you tie your horse, be sure to keep your fingers **out** of the loops. If your horse pulls back, you don't want to be caught in the tightening knot.

Halters

A halter is the *only* safe thing to put on your horse's head when you're going to tie him. A good halter is strong and unlikely to break. It won't hurt your horse if he pulls back against it, the way a bridle might. And, of course, it won't choke your horse.

There are several types of halters to choose from, each with advantages and disadvantages.

A good stout double-stitched leather halter is strong, but may be breakable. If your horse pulls *very* hard, the halter may break and free him. Then again, it may not.

A nylon web halter will practically never break. Cotton rope halters are also strong, but the hardware may break and the halter can shrink if it gets wet. Western-type, knotted rope halters without hardware are very strong, and it is highly unlikely that your horse can break one.

Tying Methods

Whenever you tie a horse, you are taking on a big responsibility. You are

---

SAFETY HALTERS

A safety halter looks like any other halter, except that the crown piece — the strap behind your horse's ears — is made of thin leather. It's strong enough for leading purposes, but will break if your horse pulls hard against it while tied or if he catches his halter on something while turned out.

Safety halters can be made of either web or stout leather. You can turn any halter that has two buckles on the crown piece — one on each side of your horse's head — into a safety halter by replacing the crown piece with one made of thin leather.

A safety halter is essential if you need to turn your horse loose with his halter on. It's all too easy for him to catch the halter on a nail, a branch, or his own hind foot. He can seriously injure or even kill himself that way. For that reason it's always best to turn a horse loose **without** his halter on.

Still, you may feel that you need a halter on your horse. If you live near traffic and your horse is good at escaping, or if he's difficult to catch, having a halter on his head can make a big difference.

If so, get a safety halter. Adjust it so it fits snugly, making it less likely to catch on things. If your horse will be grazing, you

This safety halter is made of strong web, but the crown piece is made of thin leather that will break if the halter catches on something. This is the only kind of halter you can safely leave on a loose horse.

may want to fit the halter with sheepskin pads so his constant jaw motion doesn't cause the halter to chafe. Remember, a haltered horse **must** be checked on at least twice a day to ensure he hasn't caught himself on anything.

putting him in a situation where he can't take care of himself. He must depend on you, so be dependable. Think ahead, and once you've tied him, keep thinking about him. Never tie a horse and then walk off and forget him.

Straight Tying

Straight tying, in which you tie your horse to a post or ring using a single rope, is the most basic method and, if done properly, the safest.

High and Short

When straight tying, you'll need to tie your horse high and short. "Eye-high and arm's length" is the rule.

The tie rope should be attached to a wooden post at least four inches in diameter and at or above the level of your horse's withers (about the level of his eye is a good rule). That way if he does pull back, he can't get good leverage. This also minimizes his chance of injuring his neck or back. Tying high also prevents him from getting a foot over the rope, which can cause serious injury. Be sure to tie the rope short. Leave enough slack so he can move his head without feeling too confined, but not loose enough so that he can put his head *under* the rope, which is dangerous, and may in itself be enough to make him pull. About 12 to 18 inches between your horse's head and the knot is usually good.

Be sure to tie using a quick-release knot. Practice the knot on page 71, and learn how to make it around a post or a tree trunk as well as through a ring.

Remember: When tying to a fence, tie to a post, not a rail. When tying to a tree, tie to the trunk, not a limb. You also want to be sure to tie in a spot where the rope can't slip down. Just above a branch on a tree or above a rail on a post is good.

The Rope

The rope you tie your horse with should be strong. Your horse shouldn't be able to break it with a casual pull. The weakest part of most lead ropes is the hardware — the snap, or the clamp that holds the snap to the rope. Look for a large snap and strong, careful workmanship. Ask the tack shop manager to help you make your selection.

If you'll be making a safety knot, your rope needs to be flexible as well as strong. You can get a big rope as thick as your wrist, but you probably can't tie it in a quick-release knot! Five-eighths-inch rope is standard, and is both strong and flexible. One-half inch is also fine.

In an emergency, of course, you can tie your horse with baling twine using a safety knot. For added strength, you can braid the twine. In either case, don't expect your horse to stay tied all day!

A tied horse should never be left unattended.

New Ropes

Today you can get sturdy tie ropes made of rubbery materials, like bungee cords. These increase safety, because if your horse panics they'll stretch a little, giving him the illusion of freedom. This is often enough to make him feel more secure, and he'll calm down without hurting himself. There is a stretchy cross-tie available with panic snaps on *both* ends — a good choice. It also comes in a short length for using inside a horse trailer.

A lead rope with a concealed section of stretchy material is also available, which you can use as a single tie — tying, of course, with a safety knot! And there is a new product called the Leader, which is a bungee cord lead and tie rope with a velcro-type quick-release feature.

One consideration with ties like these is that they may be too long, and, of course, under pressure they stretch even longer. This can allow a frightened horse to rear, get his front feet over the rope, or even turn around facing away from the hitch post. If you want to use a stretchable tie rope, select the shortest one you can use. If you will always be tying your horse to a well-mounted ring in a wall or post, you can use a trailer tie with a panic snap. If you'll be tying to a tree or rail, you'll need enough length of rope to wrap around and tie — at least seven feet. My stretchy lead rope has panic snaps at both ends, but seven feet is way too long for a tie rope. I make a quick release knot instead, so I can tie up as short as I want.

Cross-Ties

Cross-ties are convenient when you, the vet, or the farrier needs to work around your horse. In cross-ties, your horse has a rope attached to each side of his halter. This keeps him from moving far to one side or the other. It also holds him in the center of the aisle or stall, leaving plenty of room for you to move around him.

Cross-ties can be dangerous, though. A horse may panic if cross-tied, especially if too tightly. He can flip and fall, or become twisted in the ties. *Do not leave your horse alone in cross-ties.*

You do need a good area in which to set up cross-ties. A box stall works well, or the aisle of a barn if it is wide enough, or even an area outside between two posts. A stall mat or dirt floor provide the best footing. Avoid tying on cement floors that can get slick when wet.

Level ground is a must, as are sturdy rings, posts, and walls. And the ties you use should have one of the quick-release features mentioned earlier.

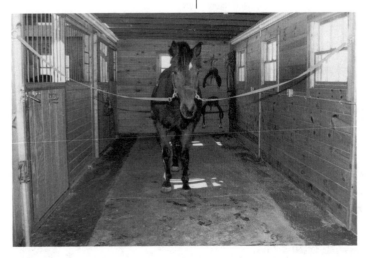

This horse stands quietly on properly adjusted cross-ties. A rubber mat helps prevent slipping.

The ties should be long enough so that you can touch the two snaps together across the open space. Hook the snaps into the two lower side rings of the halter. Your horse should feel no pressure on his head as long as he stands quietly. If in doubt, make your ties looser rather than tighter. As long as they are well up out of your horse's way and he is held in roughly the place you want him, you're doing OK.

When Not to Tie

If you have any doubts about your horse's willingness to stand tied — in general or in a particular situation — *don't* tie him. This same rule applies if there is no secure place to tie him. It's just not worth the trouble it can cause. Get someone else to hold him if you need to go away for a minute, or turn him loose in a pen or a stall.

When assessing the safety of an area where you'll be tying a horse, be sure to consider the surroundings. The footing should be secure. That means it should be dry, relatively level, and free of big rocks or loose material that might slide underfoot.

There should be no sharp objects nearby and no roof edges low enough for your horse to bump his head on.

Don't tie too near other horses. Tied horses should always be spread widely apart, so that even if both back to the very ends of their ropes they won't be able to kick one another.

Don't tie a horse inside a pen with loose horses. The loose horses may bully him or try to go under his tie rope, and more than one animal may be hurt.

Don't tie your horse near traffic — and when you think of traffic, include the neighbor who might drive into your yard and the tractor in the field that's going to pass by in ten minutes pulling a clacking hay baler.

Don't tie your horse by the reins. This means that you can't tie him in the middle of a ride, unless you are using a combination halter-bridle, or unless you have remembered to bring a halter and rope along. If you tie your horse by the reins he may break them, teaching himself that he can escape. If you tie him with the bit in, he'll hurt his mouth.

Chapter Eight

GROOMING

IN THIS CHAPTER

Grooming is an important method of checking your horse's health as well as keeping her looking nice. Be sure to groom with safety in mind.
- ✔ Review safe handling and tying rules.
- ✔ Keep your tools organized and out of the way.
- ✔ Work close to your horse's body. Don't stand off at arm's length.
- ✔ Check the hooves every time you groom.

By now you are familiar with most of the rules that will make grooming a safe and pleasant experience for you and your horse. These include the following:

- Talk and walk normally. No running, shouting, shrieking, or banging.
- Don't be *too* quiet. As you move around her, let your horse know where you are.
- Tie her safely to an immovable object at the proper height with a rope or tie that releases quickly in case of emergency.
- If there is no proper place to tie her, don't.

It is perfectly possible to groom a horse without tying her up. Just hold the lead rope in your hand or have someone else hold it. If you are grooming in a stall or quiet enclosure and no one is available to help, you can drape the rope over her neck where you can reach it easily if she moves. This is the least desirable option and should only be done with extremely calm and gentle horses.

Grooming as a Safety Measure

Grooming is one of the best ways to check on your horse's health and condition. When you do a good job, you go over every inch of your horse's body, noticing all skin problems, scrapes and cuts, places that make your horse wince when touched, and the general quality of her response to you. Grooming is essential before you use your horse. Your horse needs to be clean before you put on tack because dirt may cause an abrasion. Grooming is also essential because you need to know how your horse is feeling before you set out on her.

During times when you may not be grooming your horse often — when she is living outdoors in winter, for instance — you need to make a special effort to inspect your horse. Grooming may disturb the layer of oils that help protect her from wind and rain, so avoid using a brush. Instead, go over your horse with your hand or a rub rag. Just looking at her is not enough. Long winter hair can hide a lot of problems. And don't forget her hooves. You need to be aware of your horse's health from nose to toes in order to take good care of her.

Organizing Your Tools

Have your tools organized in a caddy or set them on a shelf or on the ground a few feet away from where you are working. It's important to keep brushes out of the way. You don't want your horse knocking them off the shelf with her tail and scaring herself. And you don't want to step on a brush and turn your ankle. Not only will it hurt, but your fall or yell of pain may startle your horse and make a bad situation worse.

If there are other horses on your place, put your horse's name on your caddy. Then use that set of tools on that horse *only*. This is especially important in boarding situations to avoid transmitting disease.

A grooming caddy helps keep tools organized and out from under foot.

Use the Right Tool

When you're brushing your horse you'll be very aware of how physically sensitive she is. It's important to remember this even though it can be difficult when you're faced with an enormous cleaning job. You may be tempted to use maximum elbow grease and the stiffest brush you can find. But underneath all that filth is a very tender hide, and your horse will rightfully resent it if you forget.

You can judge the amount of pressure to use by your horse's reaction. If she puts her head up and her ears back, swishes her tail, or moves uncomfortably, try a lighter stroke or a softer brush.

Pay particular attention to all areas that will be covered by tack: the face, behind the ears, the back, and the girth area.

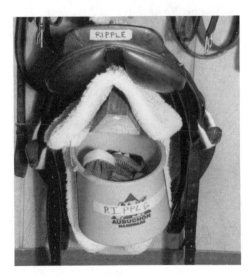

Keep grooming tools in a bucket, and label them with your horse's name. Using one set of tools for each horse helps prevent the spread of disease.

Ask your instructor to walk you through the proper order for grooming or consult a good general horse-care book.

The bony areas of your horse's body — lower legs and face — are the most sensitive. A currycomb should never be used on these areas. A stiff-bristled brush is the harshest tool you should need.

How to Groom

As you groom, stand just behind your horse's shoulder. Begin by grooming her front half with one hand while keeping the other hand firmly on her body. This is important for several reasons. It helps the horse know where you are at all times. The steady contact is calming to her. The contact also tends to keep *you* anchored in that place, which is farther forward than she can easily reach with a back foot. And if you do move, your hand sliding along your horse's body alerts her and prevents unpleasant surprises.

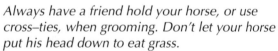

Always have a friend hold your horse, or use cross–ties, when grooming. Don't let your horse put his head down to eat grass.

Grooming the Front

While working on your horse's chest and neck, stand to one side. She might strike out with a front foot — maybe at you, or maybe at a fly.

She may also nip at you, which is less dangerous but can be very painful. Unfortunately, nipping is a casual social activity among horses — a form of play or punishment. They don't tend to view it as seriously as you will once you've been nipped a time or two. Your horse can be trained not to nip, but often it seems like a matter of reflex. Standing at her side instead of directly in front as you groom will make you a harder target to hit.

When you've finished with her front half, switch the brush to the other hand, place your free hand on her neck or shoulder, and work toward her hindquarters.

Ultimately you will need to move closer to the rear. When you do, stay close to her body.

Grooming the Rear

At first glance, working close to your horse as you groom the rear may not seem very sensible. You may prefer to work at arm's length from her. But unless you have a very unusual body with twelve– to fifteen–foot arms, your arms simply aren't long enough to put you out of harm's way. Your horse will still be able to land a good

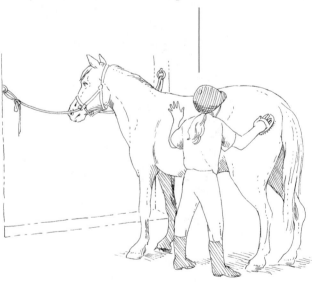

When grooming your horse, keep one hand on her body and work from the side, not the rear.

one on some part of your anatomy.

The advantage to working close is that if she does kick, she won't have much of a windup before her hoof hits you. It will be more like a shove than a blow — still painful, perhaps, but much less likely to break bones.

Never stand directly behind your horse while grooming. Instead, stand near her hip and reach, using the full length of your arm. If brushing her tail, bring it around to the side to work on. This makes it less likely that she'll connect with you if she does kick.

By standing at her hip you make it possible for her to kick you with only one foot, rather than two. One may feel like plenty, but your injuries will be slight compared to the damage a horse can do with a full windup and both hind feet.

Ticklish Places

Some horses have places on their bodies that are particularly sensitive or even ticklish. Unfortunately, the first you know about these places may be when your horse kicks or nips at you.

You need to be sensitive to her ticklish spots, but your horse needs to respect you, too, and let you groom her. If she does kick or bite, say "Quit!" Your voice should be very gruff and fearsome. Then keep on brushing. If she reacts again, be gentler and consider switching to a softer brush. Make a mental note of her senseitive spots and remember them for your next grooming session.

Use your own best judgment, of course. If your horse's reaction has been very extreme or violent, she may have some unsuspected injury. Explore cautiously with your fingers. If you suspect an injury call a veterinarian to examine her.

Handling Feet

When grooming your horse, you will be cleaning her feet as well. This is essential before riding. Both of you will feel terrible if she has a stone in her foot or some other injury and you force her to move around on it carrying your weight. Form the habit of checking her feet every time you groom.

Front Feet

To pick up your horse's front foot, stand beside her shoulder, never in front of her. With your shoulder, push her weight over onto the opposite front leg. At the same time reach down, squeeze the tendon just above the back of the hoof, and pull upward. Give her a voice command to "pick it

KNOW WHEN TO SAY "WHOA"

This is a good time to reinforce the all-important W-word — "whoa." **Whoa** is the most important word in your horse's vocabulary, for her own safety and for yours. You can reinforce the word in her mind by making her stand still with the rope over her neck while you groom her. If she moves, you'll reach for the rope, give it a quick tug, and say "whoa!" Move her back to where she was standing, say "whoa" again, and resume grooming. It's very useful and convenient to have a horse that is trained to stand still without restraint, and this is the kind of safe, simple training you can do yourself.

Cleaning the front hoof.

up" or "foot please." Use the same command every time, to help your horse learn it.

Most horses will lift their feet promptly at the slightest signal. Others will stand with their feet rooted to the ground. It may take a lot of patience, persistence, and strength to examine the feet of a horse like this.

When she does lift her foot, flex her knee so the bottom of her hoof faces upward. Hold her foot by the coronary band (the coronary band is the soft, sensitive band of tissue at the very top of the hoof). A well-trained horse will let you cradle the hoof in your hand in whatever way is comfortable for you.

Back Feet

To pick up back feet, again stand beside your horse, not behind her. Shift her weight as you did for the front foot. Reach down, squeeze the tendon, and ask her to pick up her foot. When she does lift it, gently ask her to stretch her leg backward — not too far, but enough so that you can see the bottom surface of the foot.

When your horse lifts her back foot, an automatic reflex draws the foot up into a kick position. You need to expect that and allow for it. Keep your hand on your horse's pastern, the short bone just above the hoof. If she continues to hold the foot up in the kick position, say a warning word. She should know that this is unacceptable behavior. Stay close to her hip, too. Remember, if she does kick, you want her to push you, not deliver a sledgehammer blow.

Hoof Picks

A hoof pick is the only proper tool for cleaning your horse's feet. It's been designed over many years to do the job safely and effectively. There are times when a farrier or a vet may use a hoof knife on your horse's feet, but you should never use anything sharper than a good hoof pick.

Bring the hind foot back slightly after your horse picks it up. This helps to prevent her from pulling away.

How to Use a Hoof Pick

The main purpose of the hoof pick is to remove dirt, bedding, or manure from your horse's hooves, so you can check that her feet are in good condition.

To use the hoof pick, start at the heel of the hoof. Pay special attention to the deep areas around the frog, or back, of the hoof. Stones can lodge here, and a build-up of dirt or manure in this area can cause a smelly, painful condition called thrush. You need to clean this area thoroughly. Remove all dirt from the sole of the hoof but don't *dig* into the groove. Instead, gently brush a deep groove. Be sure to make note of the hoof condition.

Farriers and Footcare

Your horse's hooves need regular care from a farrier. She may not need to be shod, depending on the kind of work she's doing, but she will need trimming about every six to eight weeks. Trimming keeps the hoof at the right length and the right angle. This prevents strain on the tendons and makes your horse less likely to stumble while you're riding. Trimming also prevents the hooves from splitting or cracking and enables the farrier to monitor any ongoing problems.

An unshod horse needs to see the farrier every six to eight weeks, or whenever a problem with cracking shows up. Cracks follow the grain of the hoof and grow upward from the ground toward the coronary band. Neglect of cracks can lead to severe lameness.

A shod horse needs a farrier's care every six or eight weeks, and whenever a shoe becomes loose or falls off. Try to wiggle each shoe every time you clean your horse's hooves. You should not be able to move a shoe. If it does move, or if you begin to hear a clicking sound from a shoe while riding, it's time to schedule an appointment with the farrier.

If your horse pulls a shoe, don't ride her until it has been replaced. This can cause stumbling or discomfort as the horse travels unevenly.

It's best to establish a relationship with one good farrier and work out a regular schedule. When timing visits, remember that a horse's hooves grow faster in the summer and slower in the winter.

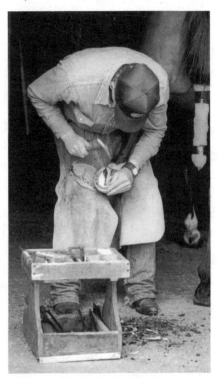

Farrier care is essential to your horse's health and safety. Note the horse's tail is wrapped to keep it from getting in the way.

Flies and Fly Repellent

Flies can be a safety problem while you're grooming and handling your horse on foot and when you're riding. As flies bite and tickle your horse she may bite at them, kick out, stamp her feet, or move around. She may even try to scratch an ear with a hind foot — with you in the middle! When she's having a fit like this, she can injure you without meaning to — she was going for the fly, and you were just an innocent bystander. But whether she meant it or not, it hurts just as much, so take precautions.

What's Biting?

Be aware of what's flying around and what's biting. In early spring blackflies and no-see-ums can cause annoyance. If they have bitten the

Different flies come into hatch at different times throughout the country. Ask your instructor or contact your county agent about what flies to be mindful of when and get a recommendation on safe repellents to use on horses.

insides of your horse's ears already and caused sores or irritation, she may react violently when you halter her or groom around her head. If you haven't caught this problem in time, you're simply going to have to make allowances for her. Use a halter that you can open and buckle on, so you don't have to stuff her ears through anything. Modify your bridle so you can do the same with it. And use great care in handling your horse's head while she has this painful problem. You must earn her trust in order to work with her safely.

In the northeast large biting flies — horseflies, deerflies, etc. — are a big problem in the late summer. Their bite is stinging and can draw blood. Horses are very sensitive to their presence and can do a lot of twisting around and kicking.

If your horse has bot eggs on her — yellow specks a little bigger than a grain of salt — you'll need a bot knife. This is a curved knife with a sharp but safe edge for shaving the eggs off without taking the chance of cutting your horse. The only other safe tool for taking off bot eggs is an abrasive brick, but that doesn't work as well.

Prevention First

To keep yourself safe and to calm your horse down, you can groom and apply insect repellent to her most vulnerable areas first — legs, belly, head, and ears.

Repellents come in three forms — wipe-ons, roll-ons, and sprays. You can cover more area quickly with a spray and without getting repellent on your hands. But keep in mind that some horses object to being sprayed.

To spray safely, begin by standing near your horse's head and spraying her body. Start with her shoulder area and work backward. You should not spray near your horse's head because you might get repellent in her eyes. Instead, use wipe-on or roll-on repellent on her head. Other areas you'll want to use a wipe-on or roll-on applicator include the belly and between the back legs. These areas are usually sensitive to fly bites and spraying alike.

To check your horse's reaction to spray, aim the can parallel to her body and give a quick spray. Don't waste the spray, but give it a moment to see how she reacts to the sound and to let her get used to the odor.

If your horse seems likely to make a fuss about being sprayed, untie her before you start spraying. Otherwise you could provoke dangerous halter pulling. Just hold the rope in one hand and work slowly and tactfully. Don't neglect to praise and reward your horse as soon as she does stand still.

There are fewer safety problems associated with applying wipes and roll-ons. But do be careful around the eyes and any broken skin, where the repellent may cause stinging.

Some horses dislike the smell of repellent and may do some head-tossing

Watch pastured horses for damage from kicking at flies.

as you try to work on the face. If this is a problem with your horse, be sure to put on your safety helmet before you begin. This will help prevent injury should your horse conk you on the head.

Work calmly and persistently. Let your horse know you aren't going to give up. As soon as she realizes her antics aren't gaining anything, she'll probably stop.

Once the repellent is applied, the biting insects will stop their attack and your horse should calm down. If she doesn't she should be told "whoa." Your horse is capable of self-control, but you may need to tell her to make the effort.

Even if there are no flies bothering you while you're grooming, think ahead. If you intend to ride out in wooded or wet country, chances are that your horse will be attacked by some kind of biting insect. You'll both have a happier and safer ride if you put on fly repellent now.

Chapter Nine

SAFE RIDING EQUIPMENT

IN THIS CHAPTER

When dressing to ride, remember these safety musts:
- ✔ You must have a well-fitted and fastened helmet approved by the Safety Equipment Institute.
- ✔ You must have boots or riding shoes with at least a ½-inch heel.
- ✔ Riding clothes should fit snugly, but allow freedom of movement.

Before you start riding, you need to be sure you have the right equipment. First, consider your own clothing. There are many choices in style, depending on the kind of riding you're doing. But there are some safety basics that are always the same — helmets, boots, and long pants.

Helmets

When riding, wearing a helmet is an absolute __must.__ It's also a good idea to wear one when handling your horse on foot, too.

There are two simple and important rules to remember about helmets:

1. If you can't afford a helmet, you can't afford a horse.
2. If you can't find your helmet, or none is available, don't go riding.

Your head is the most vulnerable part of your body. Your skull is a large, heavy bone mass. Even though it feels hard, it's also brittle, and not protected by fat and muscle mass the way most other bones in your body are.

A head injury is about the worst kind of injury you can get. Depending on the seriousness of a blow, head injuries can cause blindness, a concussion, brain damage, or death. A helmet can't prevent every head injury, but it can make a big difference. Most horse-related head injuries occur to riders who are not wearing helmets.

Think about what this means. You may tell yourself that you're just going out for a minute, that you trust your horse absolutely, that you're too good a rider to fall off, or that it's too hot to wear a helmet. But would you really want this to be the last ride you ever take? How would you feel about all these excuses if you were looking back after a serious accident?

So wear your helmet, and wear it properly *every time* you ride. You should feel naked without it.

Choosing a Helmet

Riding helmets have changed a lot in the past fifteen to twenty years. They used to be black velveteen-covered shells that made you feel as though you were slowly cooking inside them. They had rigid visors and a neat point at the back of the neck intended to protect your spinal column. In most cases there was no strap to hold a helmet on your head; at most, there might have been a thin piece of elastic.

Today's helmets are a bit bulkier. While the newest models are fairly sleek, others tend to make your head look like a mushroom or a ping-pong ball. That thickness, which may look ugly to you, is actually the visible sign of added safety. The polystyrene liner, which is what makes the helmet bulky, helps absorb the impact of a fall or kick. In case of severe impact the polystyrene foam crushes, so less of the force is transmitted to your head. In the old style helmet, the only protective element was the hard shell, which did little to protect you from the jolt of impact.

Today's new helmets are cut high over the back of the neck, so that if you fall the impact will not push the helmet into your spinal column. They have easily detached visors or no visors at all.

All these helmets fit snugly, are light and well ventilated, and are *much* more comfortable than the old hard hats used to be.

Even with all these innovations, helmets still don't cost very much, so go out and buy the *best* available. A knowledgeable tack shop manager will be able to help you choose the right style for you. A number of organizations also sell helmets by mail. Buy only helmets approved by the Safety Equipment Institute (SEI). If you happen to have an old black velveteen hard hat, think of it as an antique. Hang it on your wall as an interesting reminder of the past.

Helmets can be purchased at tack shops as well as through suppliers and safety associations. See Appendix B for sources.

A recent innovation is the SEI-Approved helmet which adjusts to fit your head through the use of an air bag. This is a good idea where a helmet is being shared by people whose head sizes differ.

KEEP IT BUCKLED

Your helmet does you no good if you don't wear it. It also does no good if you don't buckle it on snugly and keep it buckled **at all times.**

It may be tempting to unfasten your chin strap when you're coming home hot from a long ride. **Don't.** People who play with statistics tell us that most car accidents happen just a mile or two from home. I'm sure the same holds true with horse accidents. When you're close to home you tend to feel that you're in your own territory and are therefore somehow safer. It's not true. Keep your helmet on and keep it buckled.

Fit

The way your helmet fits is as important as what it's made of. Even the best built helmet won't do you an ounce of good if it doesn't hug your head.

To make sure your helmet fits properly, you must first choose the right size. Then you must make adjustments. Your helmet may come with small sizing pads that slip between the polystyrene liner and the shell and help your helmet conform better to the shape of your head. Ask your instructor to help you do this. Some of the newest, low-profile helmets come sized but should still be checked for fit.

If you have long hair, you will need to wear it in a style that does not interfere with the fit of your helmet. You don't want to adjust your helmet to fit a ponytail or French braid if you normally wear your hair straight.

This style of modern safety helmet is covered in traditional velvet. For the showring, a visor would be required.

Vent holes in this safety helmet help keep it cool. The visor snaps off easily in the event of a fall or catching.

Visors

The SEI will not certify helmets with rigidly attached visors. People have been killed when they fell off and the visor dug into the ground, causing severe trauma to the neck or spine. All good visored helmets have visors that are designed to snap off on impact or that are soft and made of fabric only. Make sure your helmet has a visor like this before you mount your horse.

Harnesses

Helmets used to come with a simple piece of elastic that snapped under your jaw. Now any good helmet will have a harness that snugs around the back of your head to keep the helmet from sliding down over your nose. It will also have a chin cup or an under-the-jaw strap. Which you choose is a matter of individual comfort. (Chin cups can get pretty sweaty and disgusting, but to some of us they feel more secure.)

Your harness will have a couple of points of adjustment. One is the lacing in the back. Your instructor should adjust this for you as she helps you fit your helmet if it was not done at the tack shop.

The other is the side buckle, where you fasten the chin or jaw strap. Make sure you understand how to adjust this. There are many different types of buckles and adjustment systems.

When adjusted and buckled on, your helmet should not move *at all*. Try some sudden movements. Give yourself a blow on the side of the head. Your helmet should remain snug and secure, as if it were just another part of your skull. You should be able to unfasten the buckle bend over and gently shake your head without losing your helmet.

Style

SEI–certified riding helmets come in many different styles, from shiny white plastic with vent holes to black velveteen, low-rider styles that look practically identical to the old hunt cap.

In addition, you can use helmet covers, stickers, and waterproof paint to change the look of your helmet instantly. Helmet covers come in racing colors, wild Lycra designs, and conservative hunt-cap black velvet.

Western Helmets. What if you ride Western? Helmets are only for English riding, right?

That has certainly been the tradition, but the heads of Western riders are not notably harder than the heads of English riders. Some Western riders have argued that since they don't do jumping, they don't need the extra protection. That's a lot like a motorcyclist insisting he doesn't need a helmet because he doesn't intend to crash! You may not intend to jump, but your horse doesn't necessarily know that. He may shy or buck.

Fortunately there is a Western-style safety helmet, manufactured by Lexington Safety Products. It's available from a number of horse-related associations (see Appendix B) and at some tack shops. The only noticeable difference between this and an ordinary stetson is the chin strap. (Early models had a considerably larger profile but the new ones are quite sleek.)

*Most horse-related injuries do **not** occur during competitions.*

This Western safety helmet has a polystyrene liner and a harness to hold it on your head. A straw style is also available.

Colorful covers and bows make it easy to vary the look of your helmet. For showing, this look is only appropriate for the cross country event.

Wear it with pride. It shows that you are an intelligent, safety-conscious rider who plans to keep on enjoying this sport for many years to come.

Footwear

Next to your helmet, what you're going to put on your feet is the most important clothing decision you will make. There are a lot of different options, but they all have one thing in common — a heel.

The heel is what helps keep your foot from sliding through the stirrup and getting caught. This can happen as you fall off your horse, and if it does, you will be dragged. For this reason, *never* ride in flat shoes or sneakers. Always wear foot gear with a half-inch or more heel.

Boots

Tall riding boots, whether English or Western, are probably the safest. A tall, well-fitting boot will tend to keep your foot from slipping through the stirrup by limiting your range of motion — your ankle simply can't straighten out enough to let your foot slip through.

Paddock boots like these offer support for arches and ankles, a good riding heel, and a nice look, too.

Regardless of style, be sure to choose a boot that fits snugly around your ankles. This gives your ankle support and keeps you riding well, even after you get tired.

You can also wear "lace-up" ropers, also called paddock boots. These short, lace-up boots are designed specifically for riding. They offer support, a good heel, and the coolness and comfort of short foot gear. These come in English and Western styles, and some brands incorporate athletic shoe technology.

Riding Sneakers

There are several brands of riding sneakers on the market today. Considerably less noticeable than riding boots for street wear, they are comfortably padded and easy to walk around in. In addition, they are not as hot as tall boots.

They do feature a half-inch heel, and are a good choice for casual riding. Do not, however, wear them with stirrups with a rubber foot pad. The rubber to rubber contact can be sticky and your foot may not come out should you fall.

Riding Clothes

Clothing for the upper body should be comfortable and should allow freedom of movement. Jackets or coats not designed for riding should be avoided. Many barn coats have a constricting arm and shoulder cut, which will interfere with following your horse's motion.

Equally, very sloppy clothes should be avoided. Long T–shirts can catch on the saddle. Western saddle horns are very apt to catch your clothing, so take extra care to wear snug clothing if you ride Western.

Protective Vests

If you are jumping or riding a particularly unreliable horse, consider a protective vest. This is a vest made of polyestyrene foam panels — the same kind of foam that is in your helmet. These vests are designed to absorb the shock of an unintended landing while giving freedom of motion. They also come with detachable shoulder pads and spine area reinforcement. They can be of considerable help in reducing your chances of serious injury should you be thrown or have your horse fall with you.

Pants

What you wear from the waist down when you ride is also important. Once again, you want freedom of motion first. You also want comfort, a non-slippery fabric, and a slim line that won't flap or catch on things.

In choosing riding clothes, be guided by your instructor's recommendations.

Blue Jeans and Sweat Pants

Loose fitting jeans are perfectly acceptable for riding. Several big name jean manufacturers produce styles especially designed for riding. Some are made of denim and easily slip over a boot. Others are made of a slightly stretchy fabric and have no thick inseam — a major drawback of regular blue jeans. This style will not slip over a boot.

Another casual wear alternative is sweat pants. Regular ones are fine, but even better are sweats made with suede knee patches, useful in helping you grip the saddle.

Breeches

For real comfort there's nothing like riding breeches. After all, they're designed for it. You can get breeches in many different cuts and styles — from the elegant flared variety you've seen in old movies to the form-fitting modern kind that are practically tights. What they have in common is that they let your body move the way it needs to, and almost all have knee patches. Knee patches not only protect your knees from bruising against the saddle, they also help you stick to the saddle when jumping or during a shy.

Tights

For super casual wear — and comfort — you can wear riding tights. These are very comfortable, but may cause chafing. Try wearing shorts over your tights for an extra layer of protection.

When wearing tights, you may experience some pinching of the calves from the saddle leathers. High boots, leggings, or half-chaps can help prevent this. Remember, discomfort affects your safety if it makes you ride poorly.

Chaps

Chaps have been worn for a long time by Western riders, first for practical protection while working in brushy country, and then for style. They're still great protection, but they have other uses for modern riders, including English riders. The roughened suede surface of chaps will give you a good grip on the saddle. Chaps can make the difference between riding out a sudden leap or landing on the ground. A lot of people wear them for schooling, because young horses tend to be unpredictable and because it's very important to keep a young horse from realizing that he can dump you.

Consider chaps if your horse is spooky or if you feel you want the extra leg protection. Don't think that you can rely on equipment like this, though, at the expense of learning to ride well. Your ability to look ahead and your ability to sit your horse securely, in balance, and without resorting to gimmicks, is what will keep you safe.

Chaps protect your legs from brush, and the roughened surface helps you stick to the saddle.

Gloves

Many riding disciplines require you to wear gloves in the showring. If the kind of riding you do requires gloves, and if you plan to show, wear them *every* day. They make a difference to your level of sensitivity, and you will do much better if you are thoroughly used to their feel. Gloves also save your nails and keep your hands from getting dirty.

Rain Gear

It looks like rain, but you're going riding anyway. What will you wear?

Your helmet, obviously. If it's a nice white plastic one, it's already rainproof. If it's black velveteen, you can get a plastic helmet cover, like a showercap, to put over it. You should *always* wear your helmet. *Never* be tempted to leave it home because you're afraid it will be ruined by rain.

Next, you're going to need a raincoat. It's best to get one that's made especially for riding. You need a coat with a roomy cut, something that doesn't make a lot of noise when you move, and that covers your legs and most of your saddle as well as your upper body.

A good combination of all these qualities is the Australian drover's coat. It has straps that hold it securely around your legs and a gusset that helps it fit over your saddle. It's quiet and it doesn't flap. This coat is available in a couple of different weights. You can also get a heavy, Western-type saddle slicker, which includes many of the same features. Breathable nylon noise-free slickers are also a good choice, especially in warm regions.

You may also want to consider wearing rain pants. Worn over your riding clothes, rain pants will keep your entire lower body dry. Again, avoid fabrics that make a lot of noise.

Do not use cheap plastic or vinyl rain ponchos. They seem like a great idea until you actually try them. You'll find then that they are awkward, bunchy, and very apt to frighten horses. They make noise, they flap, and they're very hard to keep from doing either. Yes, they're inexpensive, but far too dangerous. Don't be frugal — your safety and your horse's are at risk.

Whatever rain wear you choose, give your horse some time to get used to it, with you on the ground and in the saddle, before you head out on a ride.

If it stops raining while you're riding, dismount, remove your raingear, stow it, and remount. If you try to remove it while mounted, you may spook your horse and possibly cause a serious accident.

Tack

Finally, you're dressed. Now it's time to tack up, pausing only to consider the type of gear you're putting on your horse and the condition it's in.

If you're lucky, you'll be spending a lot of hours in your saddle. Take the time to choose and care for it properly.
- ✔ Your saddle must fit both you and your horse.
- ✔ It must be made of good leather or a dependable man-made material and it must be kept in good repair.
- ✔ Outfit your saddle with safety stirrups.
- ✔ Have a high-quality, well-fitting bridle.

The Safe Saddle

When buying a saddle, look for one made with English, American, or German leather.

A safe saddle is one that fits your horse and fits you. If it's the wrong size for your horse it may pinch him and cause him pain. This is unfair and dangerous, as his reaction may be violent or unpredictable.

If your saddle is the wrong size for you, you won't be sitting in the deepest part of the seat. You'll lose the benefit of all that expensive design you paid for. And you'll be much more apt to go flying out of the saddle if your horse shies or bucks.

Your saddle needs to sit level on its padding. Uneven padding will tilt you forward or backward and make pitching all the more likely.

A proper saddle will put you right where you should be, over your horse's center of balance. It will allow you to move in harmony with your horse. Harmony tends to make for safety, and safety should be your goal no matter what style you ride.

When you buy a saddle, shop around. There's a wide range of styles and prices available. Get the salesperson to help you find the right size. Try several models. Even saddles of the same size and type can differ amazingly in

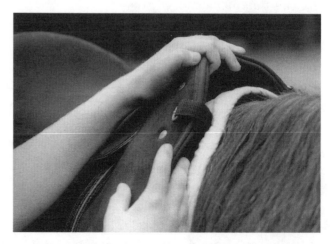

A properly fitted saddle should not touch your horse's spine but should "float" above it by at least ½" the entire length.

the way they feel. Choose a saddle that feels comfortable and that feels like it is holding you securely. You'll be sitting in that seat for many hours, so make sure it fits. Ask to take the saddle on "approval." An approval time will allow you to take the saddle home and see if it fits your horse properly.

Fitting to Your Horse

When you take your saddle home, get a knowledgeable person to help you make sure it fits your horse. Do it right away. You'll save yourself and your horse possible discomfort and you'll also be a lot more likely to be able to return the saddle if it doesn't fit.

In general, with an English saddle you should be able to see daylight from front to back, even with a rider in the saddle. This shows that your weight isn't pressing the saddle onto your horse's backbone. You also want to be sure the saddle doesn't pinch him at the withers or press upon the loins. You can't tell much about that when you're on the ground looking at an empty saddle, and you certainly can't tell once you're sitting in the thing. Expert English advice is essential.

Western saddles, too, should not put pressure on the withers, but you won't be able to look through from front to back because of the skirting. If you're buying a Western saddle, make sure that the person who helps you fit it to your horse is familiar with Western tack.

Dressage Saddles

In general, a saddle with a deep seat is safer than one that is built more shallowly. A traditional dressage saddle seems to come up around you and hug you; newer models are designed with a flatter seat. I have ridden in a dressage saddle for years now. I go trail riding in it, and I have used it in saddle-training my colt. I've found it to be a very comfortable saddle.

One popular brand is the Wintec. Available in three styles, this brand combines dressage saddle design with an extremely grippy surface. In combination with the right pair of riding pants, this saddle can practically glue you to your horse. Wintecs are also light — about seven pounds — and quite inexpensive, as saddles go. They are non-leather, easy to clean and care for, and very durable.

All-Purpose Eventing Saddles

If you're going to do any jumping, you'll be better off with an all-purpose or eventing saddle. These have a swelled flap to accommodate a shorter stirrup, making it easier to rise to the jumps. When selecting an all-purpose saddle, choose one with a deep seat rather than a flat one.

The deep seat on this dressage saddle makes for a secure ride.

An event saddle is a nice choice for general riding. The knee rolls can help you keep your seat if your horse shies or jumps.

This park saddle offers a comfortable ride, but not a great deal of depth.

Outback and Endurance Saddles

A type of saddle that is becoming more common in the United States is the Australian saddle and its hybrid cousin, the endurance saddle. These are deep–seated saddles, featuring a high, often padded cantle. Some have knee pads, and some also feature thigh pads, so the leg is held in place very securely. Intended to be used for long hours of work and travel, these saddles are built for comfort for horse and rider. This means that careful designer attention is given to balancing the rider over the stirrups, to placement of padding, to narrowing the seat, and to making the whole outfit very strong.

There are many variations of these saddles available. Some have horns, like Western saddles, and may be used in many Western show classes. Others more closely resemble English saddles. Some look very well balanced — particularly the endurance models — and others look to me as if they push the rider back a bit too far behind the horse's center of balance. A saddle like this may make a very good choice for you, but try to get the advice of a knowledgeable person before you venture out to buy one. (Wintec puts out lightweight Australian saddles, endurance saddles, and western saddles that are grippy and well-designed.)

Western Saddles

If you're using a Western saddle, the same safety considerations apply. Your saddle needs to fit both you and your horse. Get the tack shop manager and an instructor or experienced Western rider to help.

There are various considerations of style and safety. Western saddles come in many different types, developed for different kinds of work and sport. For general riding you'll probably want a saddle that avoids extremes. Choose a moderately deep seat, but not one with an enormous rise just behind the fork. The rise in some Western saddles tends to push you back against the cantle, behind your horse's center of balance.

The old-fashioned working saddle with a plain, scooped out seat puts you much closer to where you should be, over your horse's center of balance and over the stirrups. To me, a saddle like this looks much safer.

A suede leather seat can be an added safety factor, giving you more security in the saddle.

Girths

A girth has two jobs: one, to hold the saddle on, and two, to keep your horse comfortable. Thus it needs to be both strong and smooth.

Leather girths are among the strongest. Some come with elastic on the ends, which makes them easier to girth up and more comfortable for your

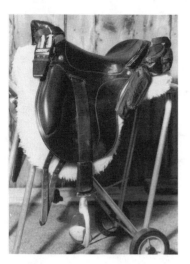

This endurance saddle is designed for comfort and safety. The stirrup is completely open on one side, and a pair of wire snips is strapped near the pommel for easy access.

This Western saddle has a nice, deep seat. Other styles may feature a back cinch in addition to the girth.

horse. There are also girths made of padded cotton or synthetic fiber. These are shaped a lot like leather girths and have the same advantages of strength and smoothness.

Cord girths are also strong and comfortable, although a little more care is needed to keep them from becoming tangled. They can be made of cotton, wool, or mohair. Do watch for rust spots, which can rot the cord.

I don't recommend web-type girths. They tend not to last long, and when they do break it's usually unexpected and total. Well–cared–for leather girths practically never break, and string girths can survive the breakage of a few strings and still remain functional. But if you break a string, it's time to get a new girth.

In caring for your English saddle, *don't* oil your billets, the leather straps that buckle your girth to the saddle. Most leather preparations encourage stitching to rot, and oiled billets stretch. Hydrophane is the safest leather care product to prevent these problems.

Cinches

Western cinches come in various materials. Mohair is traditional for string cinches, but cotton and rayon are also used. You can also find solid nylon web cinches, and even leather ones.

Cinches are secured by knotting a latigo. Your cinch may have a tongue that you slip through a hole in your latigo, it may be a simple ring, or you may knot the latigo without the tongue. Check the latigo often for signs of wear. Clean the latigo often, and condition it using a wax-based leather preparation.

The back cinch, if you have one, is usually made of leather. It's purpose is to stabilize the rear of the saddle, not to hold it on your horse. It should be connected to the front cinch by a keeper so it doesn't slip back to the flanks. There should be no daylight between the back cinch and belly, but it shouldn't squeeze.

Ask your instructor to teach you the latigo knot and how to tighten it properly.

Stirrups

One of the biggest dangers you face in riding is the possibility that if you fall, your foot may get stuck in the stirrup. If this happens you could be dragged, and seriously injured.

Guard against this by riding in boots with a heel, and by riding correctly, with heels down but not jammed forward. An additional precaution you can take is to fit your saddle with safety stirrups. Stirrups come in different sizes, and you need to be sure yours fit your feet. They should be wide enough that you can rest the ball of your foot squarely on the tread and still have an inch to spare on each side for Western, an inch and a half for

English. You should be able to move your feet freely and kick your stirrup loose instantly.

The fit of your stirrups can be affected by the type of boot you are wearing. Don't go riding in a bulky pair of winter boots that stick tight in your stirrups.

Western Stirrups

The most important thing about a Western stirrup, as with any stirrup, is that it fits your foot. You should have plenty of space on either side. The roomy shape of most Western stirrups helps ensure that your foot will not get caught if you fall. Choose a tread width that feels comfortable and that is suited to the kind of riding you'll be doing. If you can get a stirrup with a leather-covered tread you'll probably have better traction.

There is a breakaway Western stirrup on the market, similar to the English ones discussed later. It is not readily available in all parts of the country. Contact a safety organization for information on how to find this stirrup in your part of the country.

Another option available with Western saddles is a tapadero, a leather hood that covers the front of the stirrup. This offers additional protection from brush, and absolutely prevents the foot from sliding through the stirrup. Thus tapaderos offer a real increase in safety. But use a stirrup and tapadero that fit your foot. If either is too big a small foot can get caught under a tapadero and cause big trouble. (There is an option like this for English stirrups — the Dover boot. This is primarily used by handicapped riders, those with very weak legs or with impaired muscle control.)

The oxbow stirrup is currently popular in Western riding, but is considered less safe than other Western stirrups. With the oxbow, you ride with your foot thrust deep into the stirrup. This, and the narrow, rounded shape of the oxbow, make it difficult to kick your foot free.

English Stirrups

English stirrups come in a variety of styles, so you should have little problem finding a safety stirrup that suits your needs.

Foot Free Stirrups. The Foot Free Safety Stirrup can reduce the risk of injury should you fall. This stirrup has a balloon shape in the outer edge or the iron so the foot can slip out easily in case of emergency. The Foot Free Stirrup has two advantages over other safety stirrups. One, you aren't depending on a mechanical device, which may or may not work, to free you. And two, the Foot Free is heavy, so it hangs down right where it ought to be.

The Foot Free Stirrup is available in four-inch or four and three-quarter inch sizes, and comes with pads. This is probably the simplest, most reliable safety stirrup on the market, and is a wise investment, particularly for anyone who often rides alone.

The Foot Free stirrup is seldom large enough for a man. Contact the manufacturer to request a larger fit.

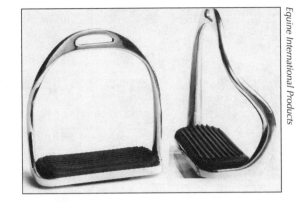

Quick–Release Stirrups. You can get other types of safety stirrups that are designed to release the foot should the rider fall or be dragged. The Peacock Safety Stirrup is the one most commonly available. The outer metal side is replaced with a thick rubber band, hooked so that it can come loose when the rider falls. The rubber band is sometimes twisted for added security.

Unfortunately, these stirrups don't always work. They can unfasten when there is no emergency — which can be dangerous in itself — and frequently do not unfasten when you need them to. In general, Peacock Safety Stirrups will not release for people weighing under fifty pounds.

Another style of safety stirrup, the Look Stirrup, borrows its design from ski bindings. Like ski bindings, these stirrups come loose only if the rider falls. They, too, need a certain amount of weight and force to make them trip, but they are used by many jumpers and cross-country riders.

Both of these stirrups share the problem of being lightweight. It's usually better to have a heavy stirrup, which tends to hang down straight at the end of the leather if your foot slips out of it. A heavy stirrup doesn't bounce around as much and you'll be able to locate it and pick it up again much more easily. It's also important that your stirrups be strong in case your horse takes a bad fall. If he lands on your leg, you don't want the stirrup to bend around your foot, or to break and stab you.

Another quick–release stirrup is the Kwik-Out. This looks like a regular iron, but the side pops out in an emergency, releasing your foot. Again, this has a stiff release mechanism and isn't suitable for very young or small riders. Also, you need to be very sure that the bar clicks in again, once you have released it, or you could face the surprise of having your stirrup come apart at a delicate moment.

Stirrups That Tilt

Your riding teacher will tell you to ride with "heels down." There's a good safety reason for this. If your foot slopes downward toward your heel, any time your foot slips it will tend to slide down and out of the stirrup — not great, but nowhere near as dangerous as sliding forward and getting stuck.

There are several stirrups on the market that are designed to help you keep your heels down. One is the Angled Tread stirrup. The angle of this stirrup helps you maintain a stable leg position and provides more traction, while placing your foot in a "heels down" position.

The Double Offset stirrup is also designed with a sloping tread

The Foot Free Safety Stirrup's sculpted outer edge lets the foot slide out easily in case of a fall.

In a fall, the Peacock Safety Stirrup's rubber band is designed to pull free from the hook.

The safety catch on the saddle bars can vary from saddle to saddle. Check the stiffness of the safety catch on your stirrup bars by flipping it up. A sharp backward tug should cause the catch to flip down so the stirrup leather can slide off the bar. If the safety catches are too stiff to allow this, ride with them flipped down. If they release easily, ride with them flipped up.

The rubber pad in this English stirrup aids traction.

🐎 *If you wear rubber-soled shoes with English stirrups, you must remove the rubber pad from each stirrup. Otherwise your foot may stick in the stirrup at a moment when you need to kick free.*

and a slope to the side, again, to aid leg and foot position.

And the new Herm Sprenger jointed stirrup features a joint in the sides of the stirrup that helps keep your heels down and aids in release if you fall.

Stirrup Pads

In addition to specially designed stirrups, you can get a stirrup pad with a built–in slant to help you keep your heels down. The B-D'Angles pad inclines your foot at the proper angle, while at the same time providing an actual obstacle to your foot's slipping forward. It also gives you better traction in the stirrup.

All of these "heels down" devices are gimmicks, designed primarily to help showring riders win Equitation classes. You should not depend on gimmicks to improve bad riding. But slanted stirrup pads are a mild, unobtrusive, and potentially useful gimmick, well worth considering.

Safety Bars

An additional precaution you should always take when riding in an English saddle is to put your safety bars *down* and leave them down.

Your stirrup leathers are hung on bars up near the pommel of the saddle. The bar has a movable catch that can be pushed into an upright position after the leathers are on. Make sure both bars are down before you mount. That way, should you fall, your stirrup leather will slide off the bar and prevent you from being dragged.

Stirrup Traction

Most stirrups are made with some gesture toward providing traction under your foot — ridges or pimples of metal. These don't work all that well. To give your foot real grip, you need either rubber or sandpaper stirrup pads.

Rubber pads come in many styles, with pimples, ridges, or bristles to provide traction. The bristle type is probably the best, but all work well. Remember, though, that they will wear smooth with use, and when they do, they should be replaced.

Bridles

The right bridle is the one that fits your horse, is comfortable, and is always in good repair.

Assuming you're using a leather bridle, the key factor to its safety is the quality of the leather. The safest leather is American, English, or German. Avoid leather from India, Pakistan, Mexico, or Argentina. Ask your tack shop manager where the leather comes from — not where the bridle was made. Some leather goods, including bridles and saddles, are "Made in

England" of Indian or Pakistani leather.

Warning signs that your bridle is in poor condition include cracks in the leather, particularly near buckles and at the bit, and rotted stitching. A bridle with either of these problems should be repaired or replaced.

Beware of making modifications to your bridle's design. I once removed the brow band from my colt's snaffle bridle to make bridling simpler while he recovered from an ear problem. I had no trouble riding until I suddenly needed to put on the brakes, and then they didn't work. The bridle was shifting around on his head so that the bit wasn't acting properly in his mouth, and he was able to ignore me. I hadn't realized that the brow band played such an important function in making the bit effective. Fortunately, he responded well to my "whoa" and no emergency resulted, but it easily could have. Don't take pieces off your bridle unless you are absolutely sure they are not vital.

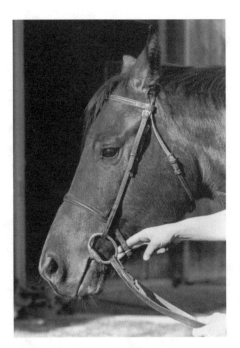

A well-fitted bridle allows two fingers between the jaw and the cavesson.

You should be able to fit three fingers between your horse's jaw and the throatlatch.

Adjusting the Bridle

The bridle needs to fit snugly and to hold the bit in place. When the bridle is properly adjusted, an English snaffle bit will be drawn back against the corners of your horse's mouth, making two wrinkles in his lips. A dressage snaffle may be tighter, a Western snaffle looser. A Western curb bit will just touch the corners of his mouth. There are many different kinds of bits, both English and Western, all of which act somewhat differently on the horse's mouth. Ask your instructor how your particular bit should be adjusted.

The throatlatch should be fastened quite loosely so there is no chance it might interfere with your horse's breathing. You should be able to put three fingers, turned sideways, between the throatlatch and your horse's neck.

The English noseband (cavesson) should be adjusted snugly, not tightly. You should be able to fit one or two fingers between the noseband and your horse's face.

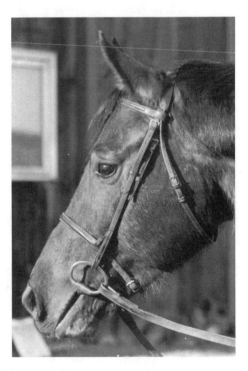

A well-fitted snaffle bridle

Hackamores and Bosals

There are also a number of bitless bridles on the market — hackamores and bosals. Don't be misled into believing that these are gentler just because they're bitless. Traditional hackamores with their shanks and bosals with their stiff nosebands and heavy heel knots can have a harsh effect on your horse's nose and jaw. Or they can offer *less* control, depending on the hackamore and how you use it. A newer "side-pull" style features a softer nose band, no shank, and no knot. Side-pulls are fast becoming a common way to start a Western horse headed for competition.

Never switch to a hackamore without getting some instruction on how to use it properly. And don't take off across country with one if your horse isn't used to it.

Halter-Bridles

If you're heading out on a long trail ride and your plans include a break for lunch, you need to consider how you'll tie your horse. You can carry along a halter and rope; or if this problem comes up frequently, you can buy a combination halter-bridle. You can find these in catalogs that specialize in equipment for trail riders. A halter-bridle has a bridle headstall that clips onto a halter. When you want to stop and tie up, you can snap your rope into the halter section, which is sturdy enough for tying and will not act on your horse's mouth.

Saddling Up

Now that you've got all the equipment you need, you're ready to saddle up. As you start, remember: Work calmly, thoughtfully, and without hurry.

Before you put your saddle on, groom your horse. Then check the pad and the girth thoroughly. Make sure both are clean and free of sticks, pebbles, or burrs. Girthing a burr tightly to your horse's back is a guaranteed way to make him buck! Drape the girth across the seat of your saddle, out of the way. If you have a Western saddle, hook the right stirrup on the horn.

Set the pad and saddle on your horse's withers and slide them backward into place. This makes all the hairs lie down in the right direction.

Smooth the saddle pad or blanket so there are no creases in it. Pull the pad up a little at the front, so it peaks up into the gullet of your saddle. This will keep the pad from putting pressure on your horse's withers and allows air to circulate.

Go over to the right side of your horse and take the girth or cinch down, lowering it gently so the buckles don't clunk into his legs.

Check that the girth isn't twisted or the blanket wrinkled.

Be sure to check the buckles or latigo on the off, or right, side of the saddle. It's all too easy to focus on the working side of things, and ride off with one of your right billets undone.

Tightening the Girth

Girth your horse up gradually, not all in one squeeze. Do it in four or five stages. Then check again after 10 minutes of riding and tighten the girth a final time. This will keep your horse in a happier mood, and make him less likely to bloat (see below).

How tight should your girth be? You should be able to get two fingers under it. There should be a hand's width between the girth and the horse's elbow, and no skin pinched under the girth. You may want to stretch your horse's front legs forward after girthing to make sure there are no wrinkles.

If your Western saddle has a back cinch, fasten it after you've tightened the front cinch. The back cinch should not be tight. It should touch the horse's belly, so he can't put a hind foot through it, but you should be able to slip your hand under it easily.

Bloating

Don't be surprised to discover that your horse has found a way to prevent tight girthing. He takes a bellyful of air and holds his breath. You tighten your girth over his expanded belly and ride off confidently, only to have the saddle slip later when your horse lets out his breath.

With your own horse and your own saddle you should be able to judge by the wear marks on the billet straps or on the latigo how tight the girth should be. How far you can pull up your girth will vary somewhat as your horse's weight goes up and down, but if you're riding him regularly you'll be aware of these fluctuations.

If it suddenly becomes impossible to tighten the girth in it's usual position, suspect bloating. A look at your horse's face should confirm this. His nostrils and mouth will seem pinched, and his eyes will have a faraway look, as he concentrates on holding his breath. You can also watch his sides, which will be practically motionless.

Lead him around in a few circles. This will help deflate him so you can tighten the girth a little more. Whenever you ride a strange horse you should assume that he is bloating and take this precaution.

If your horse has an irresistible itchy spot somewhere, you can scratch that. In his enthusiastic response he'll usually forget to hold his breath.

The classic Wild West tactic was to kick the bloating horse in the belly. *Don't* do this. It's stupid and brutal, and if he kicks back, you'll regret it. Your horse will lose the bloating habit if you are careful to girth up in four or five stages, and if you avoid girthing too tightly. Have your instructor show

Learn bridling from a good instructor and with a patient horse.

When bridling, a tall individual can hold the bridle from above the horse's head.

This method of holding the bridle is easier for short people or those with tall horses.

you how. If your horse suddenly begins to bloat, review your own habits. Remember, he is bloating in self-defense.

Bridling

The important thing to remember about bridling is not to lose your horse during the transition from halter to bridle.

You can maintain control by temporarily buckling the halter around your horse's neck; by putting the reins over his head first, and holding onto them; by slipping a strong cavesson onto your horse's head and snapping his rope into it for a moment; and by using your verbal emergency brake, "whoa."

You can also control the situation by leading your horse into his stall or a small pen before bridling him, so that if he does pull free from you, he won't be loose.

Work slowly and gently around his head, and remember to wear your helmet.

To bridle your horse, you first slip the bit into his mouth, and then bring the bridle over his ears. You can hold the top of the bridle in your right hand, with your arm coming over the horse's neck and between his ears. Or, if your horse is taller, you can pass your right arm under his jaw and hold the bridle by the cheekpieces while you put the bit in his mouth.

Cradle the bit in your left hand, and put your thumb in the corner of the horse's mouth. There are no teeth here, and you will be able to press down on the horse's gum. When he opens his mouth, raise the bit with your *right* hand, by pulling up gently on the bridle. This keeps your fingers away from his teeth. Put the crown piece of the bridle over the right ear, then the left.

Never force the bit against your horse's teeth or gums. Never bang the bit on his teeth.

Be careful as you slide the bridle past his eyes. Handle his ears gently. Fasten all the buckles and slide all loose straps into their keepers.

Be sure that the bridle is even and the bit is level in the horse's mouth. The cavesson goes under the cheek pieces. The brow band and ear piece, if your bridle has one, must not rub or pinch the ears.

The bit must fit properly — too narrow will pinch, and too wide will cost you control.

Now, put down your stirrups, check your girth, and you're ready to go.

Chapter Ten

YOU AND YOUR INSTRUCTOR

IN THIS CHAPTER

Your instructor should have:
- ✔ Credentials
- ✔ Experience
- ✔ A safe facility
- ✔ Safe, well-trained horses

You should expect to learn about:
- ✔ Safety equipment
- ✔ Handling and riding techniques
- ✔ An emergency halt and emergency dismount

Exercises in the saddle — supervised by your instructor — can help improve your balance.

Learning how to ride is *not* a do-it-yourself activity. To start out right — and safely — you need the guidance of a qualified instructor.

Instructors aren't just for beginners, either. Even if you've been riding for years, your riding will benefit from an occasional series of lessons. We all get careless, sloppy, or develop bad habits. We tend not to notice this ourselves, but an instructor will point out these faults and help correct them.

Even the best riders, people who compete at high levels in various horse sports, almost always work with an instructor. There is always something more to learn. There are always ways to refine your skills. And to get the best performance out of one horse may require different techniques than with another.

Going to an instructor should not make you feel like you are going back to kindergarten, even if you do know how to ride. It's more like going to college, and it's a wise investment. Besides the direct benefit you'll get from the lessons, your instructor can help unravel all the mysteries of tack, clothing, leading, loading, and horse behavior. Like the vet and the farrier, a good instructor becomes part of your support network, a person you can turn to for expert advice.

The Horsemanship Safety Association (HSA) provides instructors with hands-on training experience using real students. HSA–certified instructors must also pass written and riding tests.

Finding an Instructor

How do you find a riding instructor who is right for you?

Word of mouth is a good way to begin. Ask horsemen in your area to recommend an instructor. Go to a show and observe riders working at your level or slightly higher. When you notice someone who is riding well and safely, ask who her instructor is. Ask a Pony Club or 4-H leader. Ask at local stables.

You can also contact the Horsemanship Safety Association or the American Riding Instructor Certification Program (see Appendix B for addresses and phone numbers). These organizations can help you locate certified instructors in your area and, in some cases, provide training at their facility.

Once you think you've found a qualified instructor, you need to check out the instructor's facility and watch a lesson. Don't be in too much of a hurry to choose an instructor. Take all the time you need to get acquainted, to be sure the facility and horses are safe and that the instruction is good. This is a very important relationship, and one that may be difficult or uncomfortable to break off. It's best to be as sure as possible ahead of time that you'll be happy with your instructor. But don't be afraid to change if you are not satisfied after a few lessons.

Judging a Facility

Horse farms come in all sizes and shapes, and you may find excellent instructors working from very modest facilities and below average instructors at fancy places. Don't be dazzled by a lot of white paint and sparkle. Look hard at all aspects of a potential instructor's facility, and try to understand their safety implications.

The horses should be well cared for. You know by now how to judge a safe barn and pasture. See if your instructor's horses are kept the way you would keep your own. Well-kept horses are safer; and the way your instructor cares for her horses will tell you a lot about her basic attitude toward safety.

The horses should seem quiet and easy to handle. There should be a variety of different sized horses available, so that a small or large rider can have an appropriate sized horse.

Your instructor should set a disciplined tone. Hordes of kids running around and shouting, people smoking in the barn, empty beer bottles in the trash, people being allowed to do unsafe things with horses — all are warning signals that the standards at this facility are not high.

You may find situations where a good instructor is working at a facility managed by someone else. The horses may not be well kept or the barn may be unsafe through no fault of the instructor's. In this case look hard at the

It's a good idea to start taking lessons __before__ you buy a horse. A good instructor will gladly help you choose a solid horse and guide you through the process. For more information on buying a horse, see page 147.

A good rule of thumb for determining if a horse is the right size for you is that, when mounted, your foot should reach about halfway down the horse's side.

safety standards the instructor sets within the lesson itself and ask for evidence of certification. Be very sure that the area where you ride is safe.

The area where you'll be riding should have the following safety features.

- It should be surrounded by a horse-safe fence. You should not be asked to take a lesson in any unenclosed area. You should not be asked to ride within any kind of fence that is not safe for horses or humans.
- It should have decent footing. Rocks, mud, excessive dust, or hardness of the surface can all pose a hazard.
- It should be set off so you are not harassed by horses in adjacent pens.
- There should be no loose dogs or other livestock wandering around during lessons. There should be no unsupervised toddlers either.
- The gate should *always* be closed during lessons.
- Mounting and dismounting should always take place in the ring, not the barn.

Your Lessons

Once you have chosen your instructor, what will your lessons be like?

If you are a beginner your lessons will start on the ground. A good teacher will help you become familiar with handling, grooming, and tacking up. You need to know all these things. You also need the time with horses, so you can learn to understand and predict their reactions.

It's best to have your first riding lessons private — that is, you are the only student your teacher is working with for that hour. You'll get individual attention, and you won't have so many worries about learning to control a horse when yours is the only horse in the ring.

Your teacher should have a program by which she introduces you progressively to the things you need to learn. This will include emphasis on a secure, balanced seat, as well as stopping, starting, turning, and controlling your horse's rate of speed. Once you've chosen a teacher, follow the program you are given. If you're working with a teacher at the same time that you're riding your own horse at home, you may have problems you'll want to work on right away. Talk with your teacher about this and arrange to address these problems out of sequence. Or better yet, take your horse to your teacher if she'll board.

What You Should Expect to Learn

A progressive series of lessons should teach you to ride confidently at all three gaits. You will learn how to stop and turn a horse, and how to control his rate of speed.

You should be taught an emergency dismount, so that you can get off while he's still moving. Once you've learned it, you should get some practice doing it at speed.

You should be taught at least one emergency stopping method, and preferably two or three. (See page 130 for a review of several methods.)

Some of your lessons should be group lessons, so you can learn to manage while riding around other horses. You need to know how far apart to stay, the rules about passing in the ring, and what to do if someone breaks the rules.

You should also learn to ride more than one horse. Each horse is different. Each will make different demands on you and teach you different skills.

Lessons on Your Own Horse

As a beginning rider, you will start lessons on your instructor's well-trained school horses. As you learn more and perhaps get a horse of your own, you may find lessons at home more helpful. However, not all instructors will travel. *Always* put the quality of the instruction over the convenience of training at home.

Even with your own horse, the rules about facilities still apply, especially if you're a beginner. Take your horse to your instructor's facility if you can manage it. You may even want to board your horse there for a while. You can get frequent instruction, and if your instructor is also a trainer she can identify and deal with behavioral problems your horse may have.

If you must have lessons at home, create a suitable area. You can fence off a flat part of your pasture for a ring. If your horse has been trained to respect electric fences, you can even make a temporary ring out of portable electric fence. However you arrange it, do have a ring if you're a beginner.

If you're a more experienced rider, you'll be able to manage lessons in the open. Be sure to tie your dog up, put your baby brother in his playpen away from the arena, and secure your horse's buddies in a well-fenced corral away from where you plan to ride.

Instruction on the Trail

As you gain more experience, it's a good idea to go out on supervised trail rides with your instructor. She can teach you some of the rules of the trail and local hazards to look out for. She'll also watch you to see if you're able to handle trail riding on your own.

Expect riding in the open to feel difficult at first. It's more exciting to the horse than the confines of the arena. There are things to look at, grass to eat, even the possibility of running full speed. You may find that even a well-balanced school horse challenges your skills somewhat when you first

QUESTIONS TO ASK

Before taking any lesson, be sure to ask the following questions:

?   Are you covered by insurance? This is financial protection for the instructor. In order to get it the instructor probably had to meet certain minimum safety standards. Most committed riding teachers and trainers carry insurance as a standard part of doing business. Anyone who does not is probably pursuing teaching rather casually, and you should probably steer clear of the situation.

?   May I see your certification? Organizations that place a particular emphasis on safety are the Horsemanship Safety Association and the American Association of Riding Instructors. Other types of certification in clude 4–H, Pony Club, and the Competitive Horsemanship Association.

?   What is your teaching/training background?

?   Are your horses quiet and reliable?

?   What safety precautions do you take in the ring?

?   Does every rider wear a helmet? Do you?

?   What are the procedures for tacking up, grooming, and cooling out?

?   Can parents stay to watch the lesson? Where may they sit or stand?

?   How much do group, semi-private, and private lessons cost?

?   If I take a group lesson, how large a group will I be working with?

?   Do you offer a progressive course of lessons?

?   How long will a lesson last? How much of that time is mounted?

?   Will lessons be shortened, canceled, or turn into ground school in the event of bad weather — too stormy, too cold, too hot?

?   Is your instruction aimed at the showring? At pleasure riding? Gymkhana? At open shows?

?   Can I have the names and telephone numbers of other students to call for references?

?   Are there trails available I can ride on with supervision?

This last question is an important one if trail riding is part of what you want to do!

start riding out. Your instructor can help you deal with this, and give you lessons later to develop the skills you may be lacking.

When can you ride out on your own? *Ask your instructor!* She knows your skill level. She can give you tests and exercises to determine what you should try. Before you ride without her supervision, she will be sure you are a strong, confident rider with skill at all three gaits, and the ability to do an emergency stop and emergency dismount.

When planning to ride out unsupervised, be sure you have a well-trained, steady horse. Try to go out with an experienced friend rather than alone.

Learn by Doing, Listening, and Reading

One of the problems with riding, as with all physical activities and sports, is that you can't learn it entirely from books or from the words of an instructor. The words mean nothing to you until you have *felt*, with your own seat, legs, and hands, what is going on.

But there's another side to this coin, too. You can't learn entirely by do–ing, either. You can feel your horse's mouth all day long, but unless you have a knowledgeable outside observer to tell you what is going on, the physical experience will tell you little. Part of what a good teacher does is act as a mirror for you, to tell you how you look and how you are affecting your horse. There's just no substitute for this kind of information. Listen for it.

That doesn't mean books aren't useful to you, however. There are many different theories about riding, and many ways of explaining these theories. Reading about riding can help you understand what you have been doing in the saddle. Sometimes one person's words will click in your mind in a way that nothing else has yet. A lightbulb will go on, and the next time you ride, both you and your horse will feel the difference.

MOUNTED EXERCISES — THE SAFE WAY

Most lesson accidents happen to beginners, and most of them are due to instructor error. Your instructor must know how to take you through riding exercises step by step, while controlling the horse safely. Here are the safety measures to look for.

- Early lessons should be given on a good school horse, and on a longe line.
- The horse must be in side reins.
- Side reins must be unfastened while you are mounting and dismounting.
- Bridle reins should be knotted up out of the way, yet left where the rider can reach them — not twisted and held with the throatlatch as in rider-less longeing.
- The lesson horse must stop immediately at the word "whoa."
- Every time the lesson horse hears the word "whoa" he must stop, or be stopped. Then he must be allowed to stand for a moment to rest. This is his reward and reinforcement.

If you really want to develop a good seat, plan to do a lot of work like this on the longe line.

Chapter Eleven

RIDING OUT

IN THIS CHAPTER

Riding out can be one of the most rewarding experiences of horsemanship. Ensure yourself a good time, every time, by following these simple rules.

- ✔ Ride with a buddy.
- ✔ Tell someone where you're going, when you'll be back, and plan to "check-in."
- ✔ Check the weather and the time.
- ✔ Take a whip.
- ✔ Leave your dog at home.

Your instructor has said you're ready to head out cross country. What safety considerations should you keep in mind?

The first thing to be aware of is your own basic attitude. A ride like this should be fun and it should be relaxing, but that doesn't mean you can just slop along with the reins loose and your head in the clouds. You should remain alert, and you should stay in communication with your horse. That means listening to him, and it means reminding him from time to time that you are up there. When you and your horse are having fun, it's easy for both of you to forget your responsibilities. It's up to you, the rider, to keep that from happening.

Getting Ready for a Safe Ride

A safe ride begins with good preparation and planning. That is, you must be sure you're properly equipped and adequately trained. You must also know exactly what it is you hope to accomplish — a quick jaunt or a long slow walk — and whether your own condition and your horse's are up to the challenge.

As you ready for any ride — no matter how short — take your time and

For some basic principles on seeking shelter, see page 120.

think about everything you may face on the trail — from downed branches and mud holes left by yesterday's storm, to loose dogs and noisy crows. Think about how your horse will react and how you'll handle the situation. A safe rider is always ready for the unexpected. The key is to think and plan ahead.

Before you put your foot in the stirrup, here are a few more things to think about.

Take a Buddy

First and foremost, try not to ride alone. It's safer to have a companion to ride with. If you have recently moved to a new area, try to find a riding buddy who's familiar with the terrain.

Check the Weather

Some horses tend to get spooky just before a storm and others just after. Try to avoid riding out at these times.

Are there storm clouds on the horizon? Do weather conditions seem likely to produce a thunderstorm? The warning signs for bad weather will vary in different parts of the country, but unless you're an absolute new-comer you'll probably be familiar with them.

If it seems likely that a storm will blow up, *don't go far from home.* If it is actually thundering or you can see lightning, *don't go out at all!* Thunderstorms are dangerous under any circumstances. But when you are riding the dangers are at least doubled. Your horse may be frightened by the storm, giving you control problems. And if you have a horse to take care of, you may be unable to take shelter. Do yourself the favor of becoming weather-wise. Listen to a forecast, and don't take any chances with thunderstorms.

Check the Time

Now check your watch. Do you have time to get where you're heading and back again before dark? If you're not sure, err on the side of caution. It may seem like a lovely adventure to get caught out after dark, but when you're actually out there — unable to see the ground your horse is walking on, unable to see the tree branches as they slash at your face — your opinion is likely to change. You and your horse won't be able to avoid dangerous holes, poor footing, or barbed wire fences. If there are dangerous animals out there, you won't see them until you're right on top of them. Even if the animals aren't dangerous, they're likely to seem so to your horse, and startle him.

If part of your journey must take place on a road or highway, the danger is that much greater. Even with their headlights on, drivers will have a hard time seeing you and your horse. The headlights themselves may frighten your horse or momentarily blind him.

Reflectors

If it seems likely that you will be coming home in darkness, there are things you can do to make yourself more visible. You can wear riding sneakers with lights in the heels. You can wear a reflective vest. You can put reflectors on your stirrups, your riding boots, your horse's headstall, or on the upper part of his tail. There are halters with reflective tape on them, and even reflective leg bandages.

All of these measures will help. But none of them help quite as much as you may imagine. It's very hard for a driver to make out something in the road or at the side of the road after dark, and lots of little reflectors can be confusing and disorienting. It's really best to get off the road before dark.

Tell Someone Where You're Going

Does anyone know where you're heading? It can happen that your horse arrives home without you. If you're out there with a broken leg, or just plodding the five miles back, you want people to know in which direction to come looking, because your horse can't tell them!

Let someone know which way you're heading. This is important even if you're riding with a friend. Of course, you won't be able to say precisely. You may take an enticing detour or go farther than you had intended. But if you tell people your general direction, they won't rush off looking for you in the wrong place.

What to Bring, What to Leave Home

Depending on what kind of ride you plan, you may want to bring:

- A halter and rope
- Water bottle or canteen
- A jackknife
- A piece of baling twine
- A whip

A halter and rope are necessary if you plan to stop somewhere and need to tie your horse. You can buckle your halter around your upper body as you ride — but be sure that it's secure and not loose enough to catch on anything. Or you can buckle it to your saddle, or stow it in your saddle bags.

Water in the countryside may not be fit for human consumption. Be sure to bring along a bottle of fresh water if you'll be out for a long time.

A jackknife can be a life saver if your horse gets tangled in his equipment. And, if you break a rein or your throatlatch, a length of baling twine can make the disaster manageable.

Lastly, take a whip. You're not necessarily taking a whip to use on your horse. Mainly, you're taking a whip to protect your horse. If unfriendly dogs rush out of driveways and menace you, you're going to be in a position to menace them right back! If a neighbor's horse breaks through the fence as you pass, your whip can fend him off, too.

Leave Your Dog at Home

Your own dog, should you bring him along on a ride, can cause you as many difficulties as strange dogs can. He can complicate any dog problems by fighting. If you are riding on the road, he can interfere with traffic or distract you from your horse. Unless your dog is phenomenally well trained, will lie down in the ditch at your slightest word and abandon even another dog without a curl of his lip, you're much better off leaving him at home. The idea of riding off with your dog at your heels is a lovely image. The reality is annoying and hazardous for all concerned. Unless you are heading straight into the wilderness, without a moment on the road and without passing any neighbor's yards, leave your own dog at home.

Mount Up!

At this point you may feel a little like an astronaut going through a systems check before takeoff. Surely a simple horseback ride shouldn't be this complicated!

Once you've done it a few times, though, mounting up will become simple and automatic. You'll put your helmet on without thinking every time you head to the barn. You'll wear proper footgear because you'd feel uncomfortable in anything else. You'll know how to girth up and bridle properly, and your mind will be free for the adventures ahead.

Mounting

Your instructor will teach you the proper way to mount. But there are a few safety considerations to keep in mind when riding on your own.

- Don't mount inside the barn or in an area with a low overhang.
- Don't mount while your horse is tied. He is apt to start moving, and the feeling of restraint may upset him, even if he normally stands tied quite patiently. Also, you'll need to do a lot of acrobatics to untie him, putting yourself in an unbalanced and dangerous position.
- Keep hold of the reins at all times while mounting.
- Mount quickly and lightly. The most dangerous position is half on and half off, so spend as little time in that position as possible. The same is

true for dismounting. Drop both stirrups and vault off.

■ If your horse is too tall for you to mount easily, use a mounting block.

Mounting Blocks

A mounting block can be anything from a milk crate or a stump to a specially designed wooden or plastic block with built-in stairs.

No matter what it's made of, it *must* be stable. You can't have it tipping as you are standing there with one foot in the stirrup. It may frighten your horse or cause you to fall. You could even be caught in the stirrup and dragged. Be sure your mounting block is sturdy and is placed on level ground. To avoid any chance of tipping, stand squarely in the middle of it while mounting.

Be sure your horse isn't afraid of the mounting block. Strange objects often make horses suspicious. If your horse seems to have doubts about your mounting block, give him plenty of time to sniff it over and think about it before you try to get on. This will help keep him from shying out from under you.

A mounting block can make life easier. This one is sturdy and non-tippable.

Planning Your Ride

It's easy to get swept up in the excitement of going for a ride and rush to get ready. But now — before you mount — is the time to ensure you have an enjoyable ride. You do this by planning and thinking ahead of all the factors that may influence your safety and your horse's on the trail.

Your Horse's Condition

As you plan your ride and as you make your way down the trail, keep your horse's condition in mind. Try to gauge how fast and how far you can take him.

Your horse needs to be brought into condition gradually, just as you do. You wouldn't try to go on a twenty-mile hike without spending a little time getting yourself into shape, and your horse can't do it either. You need to gradually increase the length of your rides and gradually increase the amount of riding you do at faster gaits. Otherwise you risk causing severe injury, such as heatstroke or founder.

Your horse can be stressed by hot weather, too. He needs more rest, more water, and careful watching when the weather is hot and humid. Don't push your horse any harder than you'd be willing to be pushed yourself.

Your instructor or veterinarian should be able to provide you with some solid advice and tips on conditioning your horse.

A good position in the saddle is the best security when riding out.

Pause from time to time to listen to his breathing and to be sure he is sweating normally. If a very hot horse stops sweating he is in real trouble.

Most horsemen can avoid riding when the weather is severe and have no need to ride many miles at a stretch. If you want to try competitive trail riding or endurance riding, get a good book on the subject. Condition your horse carefully, using the book's guidelines. Learn how to take your horse's pulse, temperature, and respiration rate. Learn what is normal for your horse so you can tell when you are stressing him. Consult your veterinarian. Competitive trail riding can be safe and healthy for your horse if you follow the rules.

Your Condition

Be aware of your own physical condition, too. Wear sunscreen or long sleeves. Carry a water bottle so you won't get dehydrated. Carry a good carbohydrate source — granola bars are good, and you can share them with your horse! Bring along your bee sting kit if you're allergic to bee stings. If you've injured yourself previous to your ride, don't push your body too hard. You wouldn't push your horse like that and risk permanently laming him; you should have the same kind of respect for your own body.

Know the Terrain

IN THIS SECTION

The terrain you ride on will, to a large extent, determine how far and how fast you can go. Points to keep in mind include:
- ✔ Watch for slippery footing.
- ✔ Be aware of holes and make a mental note of new ones.
- ✔ Avoid deep mud.
- ✔ Keep your horse's speed under control when going downhill.

Don't ride out in unknown territory alone.

Footing

Footing is one of the most important things to think about as you ride. Is the ground slippery? Rocky? Are there holes? Is there mud?

Insecure footing will make your horse anxious. Remember, he believes that safety lies in his ability to run, and anything that makes that difficult will trouble him. He may even try to rush through dangerous footing to get away from this feeling of insecurity, and he may injure himself in the process.

The other danger is that your horse will hit poor footing unexpectedly and slip or stumble. You, as the rider, are the brains of this outfit, and you're up higher than your horse and have a better view of what's ahead. It's your responsibility to look, think, and not ride recklessly.

A good rule is to walk your horse over footing which you suspect may be dangerous.

Check carefully for holes before cantering across a field, and keep a safe distance between other riders.

Fields and Holes

When crossing an unfamiliar field you should go slowly. Big fields are always tempting and there is nothing lovelier than a nice gallop over the grass. But check for holes first, at a walk. Also keep your eyes peeled for garbage — especially broken bottles, scrap metal, and wire.

Water

Brook crossings can be slippery or unexpectedly muddy. It's always risky to attempt a crossing in a new place. The water may be deeper than you think, or there may be holes. Use good judgment. If you have the right kind of boots on, it's a good idea to get off and lead your horse across.

Never cross deep running water. The cowboys did it, yes, but a lot of them died trying. In these civilized times there's just no reason to take the risk when you can take a detour. Find a bridge or scout for a crossing place with low water.

Bogs and swamps, while beautiful, can be deceptive and dangerous. If you can find a reliable path through, they can make lovely places to ride and observe nature. It's a good idea, though, to make your first explorations on foot. Lead your horse, or leave him at home and come on your own. Your horse can get stuck in deep mud and the effort to heave himself out of it can cause strains and scrapes. Be aware, as you explore, that your horse is heavier than you are. Where you only squelch on the surface of the mud, he may sink and flounder. If an area is muddy, look for a rocky crossing place — not a rock-mud combo. In rock-mud your horse could get his foot caught under a rock and stumble.

Hills

When riding down hills many horses have a tendency to go faster and faster — "rolling" down the hill. This can result in a loss of control, a

Be extra careful when riding in areas where the ground cracks from drought. Rain can layer mud over the cracks. The ground looks solid, but when your horse steps on the concealed crack he will break through.

stumble, or a fall, depending on the footing and the agility of the horse.

You may have a problem with this particularly when riding with someone else, if the first horse in line gets too far ahead. Your horse will want to hurry to catch up, and may not pay enough attention either to you or to the footing.

When riding down hills you must both give your horse enough rein so he can balance himself, and keep him under control. Proceed slowly and keep your upper body perpendicular to the *horizon*, not the slope. Stop if you need to, rebalance, and establish control. And if going down hills gives you trouble, talk with your instructor about it.

When going either up or down hills, don't attempt anything too steep. The general rule is that if you can't walk up or down this incline upright, without using your hands for support, you had better not ask your horse to try it. When in doubt, get off and lead your horse. Managing steep hills while carrying a rider is hard work!

Pavement

Pavement is slippery, even when it's dry. While the sharp edges of your horse's hooves dig into dirt or turf and give him added traction, he can't dig into pavement. If you must ride on pavement, ride at a walk. A better choice, when possible, is to ride on the shoulder.

Your horse's shoes can make a real difference in his ability to handle pavement and ice. If you plan to do a lot of riding on pavement or riding in the winter, talk with your farrier. He may recommend borium, calks, pads, or other shoe modifications.

Natural Hazards

Sometimes the most treacherous hazards are "natural" hazards. Because they're natural they're often very easy to overlook. It's up to you to keep your eyes and ears open at all times for these not-so-obvious obstacles. You'll need to use your wits to minimize the potential danger and to help keep natural areas looking natural.

Natural hazards to look out for include:

- Farm animals
- Dogs
- Horses in roadside pastures
- Snakes
- Woodland wildlife
- Wasps
- Hunters
- Storms

Neighboring Farms

Often neighboring farmers will let you ride on their land. In return, be courteous. Shut every gate you open. Avoid trampling hay or crops, or disturbing any equipment or pipelines. Try to know a little about your neighbor's farm, too. When you ask for permission to ride on his land, ask about any areas he'd rather have you avoid. Also be sure to ask about old dumps; farms often have at least one and you'll want to stay away from them.

Ask the farmer if he has a bull. If he does, you need to know precisely where that bull's pasture is and if he is always kept there. There is no such thing as a safe bull. Even the gentlest have been known to turn on humans without warning. A bull may see you and your horse as a threat to his herd and his territory. Once you know where the bull lives, stay well away from him.

Ask the farmer if he has other horses, too, particularly a stallion. Treat a stallion at pasture the same way you would a bull.

As you ride along farm roads, watch out for cattle guards. A cattle guard is a grid-like arrangement laid over a pit. Cars can drive over the grid, but cattle won't cross them, and neither should you. Your horse could easily get stuck and break a leg. Look for another way through this fence.

Dogs

Dogs are one of the biggest hazards of riding in the country. Country dogs are usually loose in their own yards and may be very watchful and protective. Or they may just bark, which can still frighten your horse.

Think about dogs before you even set out for your ride, and take along a crop or whip. A long dressage-type whip is most helpful. You'll have a better chance of actually hitting a dog with it if you need to.

Dogs are usually more of an annoyance than an actual threat. The chief danger they'll pose to you will be when they pop out of a driveway unexpectedly and make your horse shy. As you ride around your neighborhood you'll become familiar with the local dogs, and you'll be prepared for them.

The most threatening dog is the one who comes up close and quietly to your horse's heels. This is the dog who's thinking of biting. He's also the dog who's in the greatest danger of being solidly kicked by your horse. Turn around to face a dog like this whenever you notice him, to save all of you the chance of severe injury.

If a dog barks as you pass his yard, try to keep your horse from speeding up. If you give the dog the impression that you are running away from him, he'll be encouraged to follow you.

Is rabies a problem in your area? Ask your vet if your horse should be vaccinated.

If he comes out of his yard and follows, it often helps to turn your horse to face him. Most dogs will find this intimidating and will scuttle back to the yard. You may have to turn around two or three times as you pass. Turning your horse will help you to keep him under control, as well.

Tell a following dog "no" and "stay" in a loud, firm voice. Chances are he knows those words — and even if he doesn't, the sound of your voice may bring his owner to the door.

The situation is a little more complex and dangerous when more than one dog is involved. Dogs in packs are often bolder and more likely to bite. Here you may need to speak very sternly to the dogs and show them your whip. But don't use it unless you really must, though, as hitting an aggressive dog may cause it to bite.

Be careful! You don't want to unbalance yourself, haul on your horse's mouth, or accidentally strike him. Don't hesitate to shout for someone to come out of the house and help you if the dogs' home is close by. This can save you a lot of trouble and even embarrassment. Also, you don't want your horse to kick and injure someone's dog, even if it is causing you problems.

Pastured Horses

Horses in roadside pastures are another major hazard you'll run across in your wanderings. They may gallop up behind you or alongside you, whinny, even try to break through their fences.

Try to know where in your rides you're apt to encounter pastured horses. If there are excitable horses behind weak fences, consider another route. Even if you feel confident about the fences, go to the other side of the road, settle yourself securely in the saddle, and pass by quickly. Don't dawdle there and allow everyone's excitement to build, but don't feel you must go tearing by at a gallop either. Walking is best for control — and if your horse is high-strung, don't hesitate to get off and lead him.

Snakes

In areas where rattlesnakes live, both you and your horse should be alert for them. Horses who live in snakey areas have well-developed instincts about snakes, and humans do, too. We're wired to spot them easily, to pick up snake-like sounds and motions, and to react swiftly, without needing time to think. All of this means that you and your horse are unlikely to be bitten by a rattlesnake. But being thrown as your horse shies away from one remains a real possibility. In rattlesnake country a secure seat and an alert mind become even more important to your safety. You sure don't want to get dumped onto a rattlesnake! For your horse's added safety, you may want to consider putting leather or synthetic boots on him.

Horses whose dams knew nothing about snakes may not have learned to fear them. Be doubly alert in this instance.

Wasps

Ground wasps are another unexpected hazard you may run across. Unfortunately, there's no real way to spot a ground wasp nest until it's too late. Keep your eyes open, of course, and if your horse becomes suddenly disturbed about a large insect droning around his head, take a good look at it. If it seems to be a wasp, stop, and try to retreat. If you haven't managed to stop in time, dismount and try to lead your horse away. Expect that your horse won't obey you perfectly when he's being stung all over by wasps. Just hang on, stay clear of his feet, and try to lead him away to safety.

Woodland Surprises

When riding in the woods, expect that birds, wild animals, and even humans may sometimes startle your horse. Partridges in particular make a thunderous noise when they fly up. The sound of a fly fishing rod can also be spooky. Neither you nor your horse can anticipate this. But if your seat is secure and you have good basic control over your horse, this moment shouldn't turn into a full-scale runaway.

Sometimes your horse may become frightened for no apparent reason. Remember, he has a much keener sense of smell than you do. We humans tend to get a little intolerant of our horse's fears and starts, especially when we don't see anything frightening in the area. But sometimes your horse is right. He has access to a whole world of perceptions we can only guess at. If he suddenly stops and snorts, and doesn't want to go any farther, give him some credit. Always be aware of what kind of wildlife is common to your area. If you live where mountain lions are known to be, maybe you should believe your horse when he says there's something scary out there. If the worst you might expect in this area is a raccoon, you can take a little tougher attitude and insist he go on.

Try to gauge the depth of your horse's fear. If he's just a little spooky, it's probably OK to go on. You'll want to sit extra tight and shorten your reins so you have a good feel of his mouth, but you needn't give in to him.

On the other hand, if your horse is stubbornly balking, breathing hard, and doing his utmost to turn and run, take him seriously. Turn around and go another way. Even if there isn't a bear or a lion out there, a horse this frightened is a danger to you and to himself.

Your horse is smart enough to figure out that displaying fear is a good strategy for getting him out of work. If your horse does balk seriously at some point during your ride, go somewhere else. Don't just take him straight back home. If you do, he'll probably find something scary in the woods every time you take him out.

A pasture full of grasshoppers jumping under your horse's belly can also prove hazardous.

Pamphlets regarding your state's fish and wildlife laws are available free at most police stations and Fish and Game Department offices.

Hunting Season

The most dangerous animal you'll probably encounter in your rides is your fellow human being. This is never more true than during hunting season.

Know the dates for the various hunting seasons in your area. A quick call to your state's Fish and Game Department or the State Police is all it takes. They will send you an official booklet with the dates, as well as hunting rules and regulations.

There are a lot of different hunting seasons. Some of them run at the same time, and some run one after another. Look for bird season, bear season, moose season, and the various deer seasons — bow season, muzzle-loader season, the regular season, and special doe seasons. In some areas people also hunt elk and antelope.

Deer Season

All hunting seasons are dangerous, but deer season is probably the worst. There can be hundreds of hunters out in the woods, all looking for hooved animals approximately the size of your horse.

No one should ride a horse into the woods during deer season. Even if you and your horse are swathed in blaze orange, there's just too great a chance of being accidentally shot. Every year, in every state, both good hunters and bad make tragic mistakes. Don't you make one. *Stay out of the woods during deer season and at least a week or two before and after.* If there are elk and moose seasons in your area, follow these same guidelines.

Be cautious, too, when riding on the roads, and even in your own field or riding ring. Your horse may be startled by sudden gunshots. If you do go out riding along the road, wear something bright. Go to a sportsman's store and buy a blaze-orange vest to put on over your regular riding clothes. Get an orange half sheet for your horse.

Ultimately, though, it's best to stay home during hunting season. It's just not worth the risk.

Storms and Emergency Shelter

You looked at the sky before you set out on this ride, but you've been out a long time and a thunderstorm has blown up. Where do you take shelter?

First of all, stay out of open fields. Stay away from water. Avoid sheltering under a lone tree in the middle of open space. Stay off the tops of hills.

Ideally you should find a shed, garage, or barn. Lead your horse inside, and stay back away from windows, doorways, power outlets, and water pipes.

If you are near the woods, take shelter in an area of low underbrush. Try to avoid the tallest trees, which are likely to attract lightning.

A cave or an overhanging bank is also a good place to shelter.

On the Road

IN THIS SECTION

Riding on roads can be an enjoyable experience as long as you keep these principles in mind.

- ✔ Expect drivers to be ignorant about horses.
- ✔ Ride on the right, unless the left side of the road is wider and safer.
- ✔ Ride on the shoulder.
- ✔ Ride single file.
- ✔ Stay alert, and dismount if appropriate.
- ✔ Ride a calm, experienced horse.

Roads can be the most dangerous place to ride your horse. But unless you are very fortunate and live in the midst of a maze of woodland trails, you will probably have to ride on roads sometime. You and your horse can share the roads with cars and trucks if you are careful and sensible.

Which Side?

Which side of the road do you ride on? Most of us have been taught to walk on the left side of the road. But on your horse, you are not considered a pedestrian. You are traffic, and you should ride on the right, the same side that you would drive a car.

This means that oncoming traffic will be on the other side of the road, and traffic coming from behind you will be on *your* side. In general this is safer, because the instinct of a horse when startled from behind is to rush forward. When faced with something frightening that's coming at him head-on, your horse will want to turn and head the other way. If you were riding on the left, facing the traffic, he might turn into the path of the oncoming vehicle rather than away from it. This could lead to a severe accident.

But this is a grey area. Some people prefer to ride on the left. Check with your instructor about which side you should ride on — it may be a matter of state law.

There is one universal rule, though: All other things being equal — footing, pastured horses, other hazards — always ride on the *outside* of curves.

Single File

When you are riding on the road in a group, go single file. It's not as easy to talk that way, but don't be tempted to ride two or three abreast, even on a quiet country road. The better the time you're having and the better the conversation, the less apt you are to hear a car coming. On a nice back road, the driver of the car won't be expecting to meet somebody any more than you are.

Be alert as you ride along the road. Listen for the sound of approaching cars. Figure out which direction they are coming from. If the approaching vehicle sounds as if it may be large or very noisy and possibly frightening to your horse, look around you. Is there a place up ahead, or just behind you, where you can get your horse well off the road until the scary vehicle has passed? Get to it and wait there or dismount and hold your horse.

If not, assess the situation and your horse. If a school bus or a milk tanker is roaring toward you, it's best to hop off, take firm hold of the reins near your horse's bit, and turn his head away from the road.

Most traffic, fortunately, is not that terrifying. If you have selected your horse carefully and wisely, he probably isn't too bothered by cars. Stay mounted and just keep him walking. In fact, pick up speed slightly. Don't go from walk to trot, but try for a little faster walk.

Take a slightly firmer grip on the reins, especially if you have been going along very loose and relaxed. There may be something about the approaching vehicle that you can't hear or see yet — a flapping tarp, a barking dog in the back of a pickup — that could frighten your horse.

Ride on the right side of the road leaving at least one and a half horse lengths between you and the rider in front of you. When a vehicle passes, make sure you have your horse well in hand and get as far off the road as possible.

Some drivers may make it difficult for you. Some may beep their horns in friendly greeting, or because they want to see your horse jump. Others may downshift noisily as they slow to pass you — a well-meant courtesy that causes more trouble than simply passing at normal speed would do. Still other drivers, not understanding the traffic rules involving horses, may creep along behind you, unwilling to pass at all. Every time a car approaches you need to settle yourself securely in the saddle, and make sure you can take control quickly should something unexpectedly startle your horse. Don't tighten up too much on the reins, though. This will signal your horse that you expect something bad to happen. Be calm, but be prepared.

When riding in large groups, have experienced riders in the front *and* the back of the line to act as flagmen, to slow and control traffic. These riders should wear orange vests or other bright clothing and carry flags to direct traffic with.

Remember that pavement is slippery. If you want to go faster than a walk, ride on the shoulder and keep an eye out for holes and culverts, wire, and trash.

Crossing the Road

When crossing a road on horseback, follow the same rules you'd use when on foot. Cross where there is good visibility — a nice open straightaway, not a blind corner or where overhanging trees block the view. Look both ways. Listen for oncoming vehicles. Move briskly. Don't dawdle in the middle of the road.

If you're riding with others, all of you should cross the road at the same time. This gets you across in less time than it would take if you went single file. It also prevents having some of you on each side on the road when a car comes along. This is confusing for drivers and also dangerous, especially if one horse is worried about being left behind and tries to cross over to join his pal. He may not notice oncoming traffic.

Bridges

Some horses are frightened of bridges, which is perfectly reasonable from their point of view. Bridges come in all sizes, shapes, and circumstances, and how you deal with your horse's reluctance will depend on all of these.

If your horse is afraid of a particular bridge, be willing to get off and lead him. Lead him back and forth several times, until he seems calm. Then ride back and forth. You will have less trouble the next time you come to this bridge, and the time after that you'll probably have no trouble at all.

On a larger, main road bridge with a steadier flow of traffic, don't linger doing a training program. Get off and lead your horse across quickly but calmly.

Riding in Company

When you ride out with others, you have more than your own horse to think about. You have your friends' horses, your friends' level of skill, and their attitude toward safety to consider.

IN THIS SECTION

Keep group rides fun and enjoyable for everyone by following these simple safety rules.
- ✔ Ride at a speed that's comfortable to the **least** skilled rider or **least** trained horse in the group.
- ✔ Keep proper spacing between horses — at least one and a half lengths.
- ✔ Don't horse around.
- ✔ Be aware of any horse in poor condition. Go slowly enough to keep that horse from being overstressed.

Take Care of Others

Ride at a speed that's comfortable to the least skillful rider in your group. There's nothing more frightening or dangerous for novice riders than to be swept along by a group or a green horse, and to be forced into situations with which they can't cope. If you are a good rider it is your responsibility to look out for those less skillful. Save your stampedes for another time when you are with friends who ride at the same level you do.

If you are that novice rider, it's your responsibility to speak up. Don't let others put you in danger through ignorance or through bad manners. And don't be ashamed of admitting that you're new at this and less skilled than your friends. You'll learn, if you live long enough! Make sure the others give you that chance.

Take Care of the Horses

As you look out for the poorest riders, be careful too of the well-being of the horses. All horses out in a group will go farther and faster than they might alone. They may push themselves harder than they ought to, especially old, fat horses who don't get this kind of treat often. Your neighbor's plump pony may seem to keep up well, but he'll pay for it in the end, unless someone wiser than he makes him take it easy and gives him time to rest. That's your responsibility if you're his rider. It's also your responsibility if you're the only rider in the group who notices a horse in some distress.

Keep Back

The most important thing to remember when riding with a friend is to keep your distance. When following in single file, keep at least a one and a half horse's length gap between your own horse's nose and the other horse's rump. You should be able to see the hind hooves of the horse ahead of you by looking between your horse's ears. This is doubly important if the horse in front of you wears a red ribbon in his tail, the time-honored sign that he is a kicker.

But take this precaution even if there is no red ribbon in sight. Most people don't take the time to put a ribbon on their horse's tail when heading out for a casual ride, and some people aren't familiar with the custom. Your friend may not even realize that her horse is a kicker.

Out on the trail, older or more experienced riders should be watchful that riders keep a safe distance and are riding at a speed that is comfortable to the least skilled rider or horse.

And, of course, any horse can kick at any time. Even if the two horses are old pals or stablemates, the lead horse may be in a bad mood, may feel threatened by your horse's nose so close behind, or may simply be feeling playful. If he does kick out, his reasons won't matter. Your horse could be injured, and you could be kicked as well.

Riding side by side is where *you* are most apt to be kicked by a friend's horse. Keep a good distance between you — about twelve feet is a good rule.

Group Think

Another danger of riding in company is the group mentality that can develop among riders as well as horses. There's pressure to do what everyone else is doing, even when it's dangerous. There's a temptation to go fast or be reckless. And when a group of horses moves fast, it is very difficult for anyone, especially a novice, to get her mount to do something different.

When riding in a group, keep in mind that your horse is a herd animal. He likes being in a group of his peers, and he's probably having a marvelous time.

Take care that he isn't having too good a time. He should remember that you are on his back and that you are in charge. Otherwise he may start playing by horse rules, not human rules — biting, kicking, jostling and racing — which is hazardous for you and your friends.

Speed

The time your horse is most apt to forget you're up there is when speed is involved. The faster the gait, the more exciting it's apt to be for him. Horses have a built-in love of traveling together at speed, of racing and jostling for position. You could suddenly find yourself in the middle of a stampede, and your chances of getting your horse to pay attention to you will not be great. When entering or leaving a group, be sure to ride at a walk or slow trot so you don't set off a chain reaction among the other horses.

And don't canter or lope in a group unless all riders are very experienced. If you do want to canter, follow these rules so no one gets hurt.

- **Let others know.** Announce your intention to canter or lope before-hand, and make sure everyone riding with you agrees. If there is an unskilled rider in the group, don't canter.
- **Know where you are.** Don't start cantering when the footing is bad. If the footing becomes bad up ahead, consider whether you'll be able to slow down in time. Count on the fact that it takes longer to put on the brakes when cantering in a group.
- **Pass all hazards before cantering.** If you have to pass a yard with dogs or a field with fenced-in horses, wait until you're past before cantering. A shy at speed, in a group, can spell disaster.
- **Don't canter or lope down the middle of dirt roads** unless they are truly abandoned dirt roads. Make sure you can see in both directions. Slow down and move toward the right shoulder as you approach curves.

Jumping

IN THIS SECTION

Jumping requires skill, discipline, and planning. Before you attempt any jump, make sure you:

- ✔ Have proper training
- ✔ Scout the footing carefully
- ✔ Look out for wire
- ✔ Inform others in your group of your intention and make sure they're comfortable with it

When you're out riding cross-country, you'll encounter obstacles on the trail — logs, stone walls, etc. Some of these can be jumped . . . depending.

Jumping Know-How

Do you know how to jump? If you don't, get your instructor to give you some lessons. You don't need show jumper training to hop your horse over a small log on the trail. But you do need some know-how.

The Landing Area

Before you attempt a jump, know what the footing is like on both sides of the obstacle. Ride up at a slow gait and look carefully at the landing area *before* you commit your horse to jumping any unfamiliar obstacle. It's best to get off and look for sticks, holes, branches, wire, sharp-looking stones, or slippery footing such as mud or ice.

Jumping No's

When out riding, it's always tempting to jump just about any obstacle in your path. However, there are two obstacles to be especially leary of — wire fencing and stone walls.

You should *never* jump a wire fence, no matter what height. Horses have a hard time seeing and judging the height of wire fences. If your horse misjudges he could be severely injured. Or, even worse, both of you could become tangled in the fence together.

A stone wall in good repair can be jumped, provided it is not too high for your horse and your level of skill. If it is slumped and spread over a wider area, you'll probably be better off looking for a place to step over it or go around it. Watch out for stones turning under your

Small logs on the trail make good practice jumps. Leave plenty of space between horses.

horse's hooves and for hidden, leaf-filled holes.

Watch out, too, for old barbed wire on the ground. Stone walls were once used as fences. When barbed wire became available many farmers strung some up along their old stone walls for reinforcement. By now the fence posts may have rotted out and much of the wire may be hidden in the leaves. Look for it, and look along the stone wall for old fence posts and for rusty stubs of wire on trees *before* you try to cross with your horse.

Jumping in a Group

Jumping and galloping are dangerous for novice riders and it's best not to engage in these activities while riding with them. If you're with a group, make sure jumping is OK with all members of the group. Remember, other people's horses may be swept along by the excitement and if they're not good at jumping, this can be a very dangerous situation. Make sure that people who don't want to jump have their horses well under control before you take off and offer them an alternate route. You don't want them to be left stranded on the other side while the rest of the group goes merrily on its way.

When You Get into Trouble

Despite all precautions, you will have the occasional difficult moment out riding with your horse. The world is full of startling things, and some of them will take you and your horse by surprise.

Shying

Your horse's reactions are swift, and because he's so large, they can be violent. You may not get any warning. He may just leap sidewards in mid-stride, a difficult moment for even a very good rider.

The first thing to do, of course, is to keep your seat. It will help if you have been riding correctly — relaxed, in balance, with your knees pointed forward, your heels down, your seat deep in the saddle, and your buttocks relaxed. That's the only way I know to stay mounted. You can grab for your horse's mane, but this tends to pop you too far forward. And the first leap is often so quick and violent that you'll miss.

Next, you need to get your horse under control. Sometimes one leap will be all he'll do, and you can just pull yourselves together and continue on your way. Other times he may be genuinely startled or frightened, or he may take the opportunity, while you're shaken and unbalanced, to run away.

Shorten your reins and say "whoa!" in a firm but quiet voice. You don't want to scare him anymore by raising your voice or sounding worried. Once he's stopped, turn him around to face the thing that startled him. This is not the time to worry about finesse. Just pull him around and get him stopped. Take a moment to settle yourself in the saddle, and let him calm down. Then urge him on.

Calming Your Horse

It's very important to give your horse time to think when something has frightened or upset him. Make him stand still facing the fearsome object, speak reassuringly to him, and just wait for a minute. As soon as the "run" signal stops flashing in his brain, your horse's eyes will seem to clear. He'll realize that crouching menace is just a pile of hay or an old tire. At this point he'll give a sigh, his neck will lower about an inch, and he'll start looking around at other things, or trying to snatch a bite of grass. Give your horse every opportunity to be sensible, and often he will.

Making Him Face His Fear

Whether you should urge your horse to go very near the object that frightened him depends on the situation and your knowledge of your horse. Some horses shy out of sheer high spirits or because a poorly trained rider scared them. Others know it's a chance for them to get the upper hand. If you sense your horse is in this kind of mood, it's best to establish your dominance. Urge him strongly forward with your legs, give him a tap with the whip if necessary, and make him go close.

If the object is truly new and frightening, or if the footing is uncertain — ice, mud, shale, or pavement — don't make an issue of it. One of the advantages of being human, and smarter than your horse, is that you can pick your fights. Get your horse moving again, but make a wide detour. And make plans about how you will help your horse overcome this particular fear.

An important and useful strategy is to dismount and *lead* your horse up to the scary thing. Dismounting is not an admission of defeat. It is one strategy a flexible and intelligent horseman can use to win in the long run.

Keeping Control

There are other times when it is wisest to hop off and control your horse from the ground. If he's terrified of trucks and you see a school bus or a road grader coming toward you, get off his back immediately. This is not a moment to worry about keeping his respect. Your horse is probably too frightened to notice if you're on his back or not. You'll have a better chance of controlling him from the ground, and controlling him will be the only thing on your mind. You won't have to worry about falling off, too. It's always best when your horse is really frightened to separate the issues and deal with only one thing at a time.

Before attempting your first ride out, be sure to have your instructor teach you an emergency dismount.

Keep a good grip on the reins as you dismount. If you have time, bring the reins over his head and hold them in both hands, in the correct leading position. Remember to stay between him and the object of terror, so he isn't stepping all over you. At a time like this, you'll be glad your riding instructor taught you how to dismount quickly, with your horse in motion.

Runaways

The best time to stop a runaway is at the moment when it starts. To do this you must ride alertly, you must understand your horse's reactions, and you must take quick action.

The true hysterical runaway is rare. Most situations where you'll need to stop a horse quickly involve:

- The horse shying and running a short distance, without any real intention to go far.
- A horse heading toward the stable and deciding to get there a little more rapidly than you would like.
- Horses racing one another — as in a group riding situation that gets out of hand.

Prevention is possible most of the time. Barring the truly unusual, like a meteor landing next to you, you can usually predict or prevent your horse's shy, ride it out, and regain control quickly.

To prevent a horse from running home with you, make it a rule to always walk the last mile. He'll still want to hurry, and many horses will use every opportunity to take advantage of you at this time. Be alert, and don't let the horse speed up even a little bit. A flat–footed walk is what you must demand. Anything faster has the potential to snowball.

Horses in groups are harder to control than horses alone. When riding with friends, you must be extra cautious. (See page 124). Horses cantering together — sometimes even trotting — have a natural inclination to race one another. You must prevent this if you are to stay in charge of the situation.

Other riders may not share your concern for safety, though. Or they may not have the same degree of control over their horses.

If your horse does manage to go beyond the first few strides of a runaway, there are three basic ways to stop him. (Your instructor should discuss this issue with you before you go out riding on your own. If she hasn't, ask.)

The quickest, strongest way to stop a horse is a pulley rein. Briefly, you shorten the reins, brace one hand, holding one rein against the horse's neck, then pull *up* and *back* on the other rein. This is a powerful rein effect. Talk it over with your instructor, and practice the motions under guidance until you understand them thoroughly. The pulley rein is useful for stopping your horse very promptly, especially in wooded or crowded situations where you might endanger yourself or others by swerving.

Another method is called doubling. To double a horse, sink your weight in your heels until your seat is very secure. Shorten the reins and brace them on your horse's neck with one hand. Reach *below* with the other hand, take hold of one rein, bring the horse's head around toward your knee, and wait. He'll straighten his body out in line with his neck, and as he does will bring himself down to a trot.

Avoid doubling where the ground is steep or slippery, or where there is no room to maneuver.

If your horse isn't really running away, but is going faster than you would like, you can use the tug and release method.

Give a short, sharp tug on both reins. After the tug, release for a second. That can be a terrifying idea if your horse is going like a freight train. But the release is just as important as the tug, or even more so. When you let the reins slacken for a moment, your horse can't lean on the bit. He has to back off a little and rebalance himself. Meanwhile you're giving him another tug, and another, and before he knows it he's under your control again.

Coming Home

Always walk the last mile home. This prevents your horse from developing the annoying habit of trying to run away with you on the way back to the barn and it lets you bring your horse in cool. You will want to have your horse cool before turning him loose anyway. Walking home saves you the boring work of walking him on foot.

It's also good for your horse's mind to end each working session on a note of calm and relaxation. That is the impression he'll carry with him overnight, and it will help give him a better attitude the next time you saddle up.

When you get home, unsaddle, noting as you do whether there are any bumps underneath the saddle blanket. As you release the girth, be careful to keep it from banging against your horse's legs.

Good equipment, good instruction, a well-trained horse, and a quiet, thoughtful attitude will insure a lifetime of safe, pleasurable riding.

You can help your horse cool off by sponging his legs, neck, and stomach. Allow his back to cool naturally before washing off the sweat, or you may cause bumps. Don't use cold water straight from the garden hose. If you have left a bucket of water in the sun, that will be more

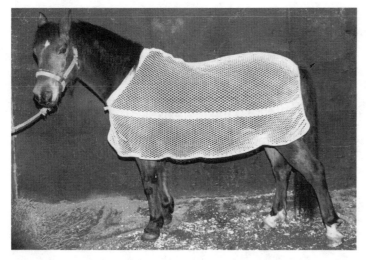

A mesh anti-sweat sheet helps prevent chilling, or can serve as an insulator under another blanket.

comfortable and less shocking.

Your horse will enjoy a good rubbing on the withers, neck and chest, and a brief grooming to remove sweat marks. Give his back a good currying or a rub with a scratchy towel.

He should be cool when you turn him loose. Check by feeling his chest. He should feel about as warm as he does normally. If he's hotter, walk him cool. Let him have a few swallows of water if he wants it, but don't give him free access to water — or a feeding of grain — until his body feels normally cool and his sweat is drying.

Check your horse's feet for any stones or debris. Notice if he has any scratches on his legs or nicks on the backs of his pasterns where he may have stepped on himself. If he's overstepping, he needs farrier attention.

Then tell him thank you and give him a treat in a bucket before you leave him. As simple as this sounds, it's important. It will help keep good feeling between the two of you. Many horses don't particularly love to work. But even if your horse is quite lazy, he can keep a good attitude toward you if he gets plenty of appreciation and rewards. Remember, your horse isn't going to understand a Hallmark card. He wants material rewards, so make sure he can taste and touch your thanks.

Chapter 12

TRAVELING TO AND PARTICIPATING IN COMPETITIONS

IN THIS CHAPTER

When shipping your horse:
- ✔ Be sure the trailer is in good condition.
- ✔ Have a knowledgable driver.
- ✔ Take your time.

Chances are if you have a horse, you're going to want to compete him at a big show, trail ride, combined training event, gymkhana, open show, or play day.

These events can be nerve-racking at first. Your horse is in unfamiliar territory, with a lot of excitement all around. You're excited too, perhaps tempted to try things you aren't really prepared for. And there are all the other people and their horses to watch out for, too.

Long before show day, there are two simple steps you can take to make competing a safer and happier experience for both you and your horse.

- ■ **Be sure your horse has all necessary vaccinations at least two weeks before the show date.** A lot of strange horses crowded together makes an ideal environment for passing on sickness. For this reason your horse will not be allowed on most show grounds without a health certificate. Make sure you know the health certificate laws of your state and those of any state you travel to for events.

- ■ **Line up your transportation well in advance.** Know how you're going to get to the show, and make plans for arriving early. Most mishaps with loading and trailering happen because people are in a hurry and feeling frantic. Horses pick up on these emotions very quickly — and your horse won't know you're acting wild because you're half an hour late. He's going to assume there's something really wrong!

Many shows — especially combined training shows — will require trainers to sign a waiver allowing you to compete.

If trailering your horse across state lines, check with the appropriate state agriculture departments about health requirements.

133

The Trailer

To safely haul your horse you need:
- ✔ A safe trailer in good repair
- ✔ A suitable van, truck, or vehicle with heavy shocks and springs and good mirrors
- ✔ A driver who has plenty of safe experience handling live-weight loads

Aluminum trailers are generally the safest type of trailer and well worth the extra expense.

Whether you are buying your own trailer, renting, hiring a trailer or van with driver, or just riding along with a friend, it is *your* responsibility to check the trailer thoroughly first. The older the trailer, the more thoroughly you should check it.

In many states the trailer you use must have an up-to-date inspection sticker in order to be on the road at all. But don't assume that means the trailer is in perfect shape. Go over it thoroughly to be sure it is safe. If you don't know what you're looking for, take it to a shop or garage that builds or repairs them. Have them inspect the trailer with you, and ask about all the items mentioned below.

Check to see that directionals and back-up lights work. Make sure the tires are properly inflated, and that they have plenty of tread left. Look at the hitch and at the safety chains. Safety chains should be fastened whenever the trailer is hitched to the towing vehicle.

Check all wiring. Sometimes when the wiring is in disrepair your horse can actually get a shock from the sides of the trailer. You can also be delayed by darkness if your trailer lights don't work.

The trailer should have a non-slip rubber mat on the floor. Lift that and inspect the floorboards to be sure they are sound.

Next, check for the kinds of things you have looked for in your barn and pasture — protruding metal your horse might cut himself on, splinters of wood from the partition, broken tie rings. Be sure to check the condition of the floor. Look for splinters and weak spots. You'll want to put a mat down for extra cushion. An inch or so of shavings on top of the mat adds cushion and absorbs urine.

Many states require drivers to have a commercial license to haul someone else's horses. Contact your state's department of motor vehicles to learn your state's regulations.

Some horsemen like partitions and front panels to be padded. They believe it gives the horse a little extra protection. Others don't use it because it encourages leaning in some horses. If your trailer has padding, make sure it is in decent repair. If there are holes in the stuffing, check — cautiously! — to be sure that hornets have not nested there.

There should also be a rump chain that you can snap behind your horse.

It should be strong, well attached and it should fit your horse. A chain that fits a pony obviously won't fit a big horse. Ask your instructor to demonstrate a good fit. A rubber or plastic tube should be slipped over the chain, so it does not chafe your horse's haunches.

The ramp, if there is one, must also be strong, and fitted with treads to reduce slipping.

The tailgate must close properly, with strong, well-oiled bolts. Be sure the bolts also open relatively easily. You must be able to get your horse out once you've gotten him in there.

An escape door towards the front of the trailer lets you check on him, soothe him, or feed him a treat without opening the tailgate and making him think you're about to let him out.

The trailer must also be tall enough to accommodate your horse's height with some room to spare. For this reason cattle trailers aren't suitable for transporting most horses. You may be able to use one to move a pony, though.

The horse should be able to back up against the rump chain before the rope tightens on his head.

The Vehicle

The towing vehicle needs to be of a size and strength to match the trailer. A full-size pickup truck is ideal for a two-horse trailer. The towing vehicle needs heavy-duty shocks and springs. It should have excellent, well-maintained brakes. Mirrors should be large, with angle insets to cover blind spots and extending well out to the sides for good visibility.

It's a good idea to have *flares* and a CB radio or *telephone* in the truck when you are hauling horses, particularly for long distances.

The Driver

The person who drives your horse must be responsible and experienced. Experience driving a car or even a pick-up truck is not enough. The weight and length of a trailer makes this type of driving very different. Turns are much wider. The brakes need to be applied carefully and gradually. *Do not* take off with your horse and trailer the morning after you get your driver's license. If you expect to drive your own horse trailer in the future, set up some cones in the pasture and practice with the trailer empty. Make sure you can back and park your trailer, too, or you may be stuck, and embarrassed, when you pull into the horse show grounds.

The driver must be prepared to go as slowly as is necessary in order to give your horse a smooth ride. The driver should be accompanied by a

Don't accelerate out of a turn until the trailer is absolutely straight behind the truck.

passenger who is experienced at handling horses. This is especially true if the trailer holds two or more horses. In case of emergency, the horses may need to be unloaded, and it can be vital to have enough people to handle them all. A good rule of thumb is to have two people to unload each horse. You also need one person to hold each horse after it's unloaded.

Traveling Clothes

Before you load your horse, put his traveling clothes on him. These include leg protection and bell boots at a minimum.

There are many different kinds of bandages and shipping boots, and the variety may be confusing. Remember what they're for — to protect your horse's legs and hooves against injury. Even if the trailer is driven carefully, your horse is bound to be jolted somewhat. He can step on his heel or coronary band, cut a leg, or damage a tendon. He needs padding, and he needs protection for the upper parts of the hoof. The leg protector you use should do both these jobs.

Shipping boots are the easiest to put on, and since they cover both leg and hoof in one smooth unit they are also safest. If you intend to trailer your horse frequently they are a good investment.

If you're going to use bandages, you also need pads — called leg wraps — to go underneath them. Leg wraps are thick and either quilted or fleecy. You wrap them around your horse's lower leg, covering the area from the knee to just below the coronary band. Then, quickly, wrap a stretch bandage around the leg wrap. It takes practice to learn how to do this without dropping either the bandage or the wrap.

Wrap the bandage smoothly and snugly. It should be tight enough to stay on, but not tight enough to impair circulation. If you aren't sure how to tell you've done it right, ask someone with experience to check for you.

Whether you choose shipping boots or bandages, do practice putting them on before the day you ship your horse. You need to know how long it will take you, and your horse needs a chance to get used to these strange things on his legs before he has to start thinking about getting into the trailer.

Blankets

If you're going to use a blanket, be sure your horse is used to being blanketed well before time to load. A blanket isn't always necessary for shipping. It depends on the weather, the trailer, and the horse.

If the weather is cool, if you're going a long distance, or if the trailer is drafty, a blanket is a good idea. No matter how nice your trailer may be, it's

Names for and terminology about leg protection vary from region to region. Ask your instructor to explain how best to protect your horse while hauling.

still a metal box being towed through the air at high speed. There will be drafts and a chilly feeling. Use the weight of blanket suitable to the conditions. In warm weather you may not use a blanket going *to* an event, but might put one on for the trip home, when your horse is tired and possibly a little damp.

Halters and Helmets

You may want to fit your horse's halter with fleece pads. These attach to the halter with velcro. They keep the halter from chafing your horse's face. They also protect his face, should he bump against the side of the trailer.

An additional protection is a leather head bumper — basically, a helmet that attaches to the halter. If your horse throws his head up or rears inside the trailer, the head bumper keeps his poll from being injured. If possible, get a head bumper that can be attached or removed without taking the halter off.

It's a good idea to take along an extra halter when trailering. If the horse pulls and breaks the one he is wearing, a spare is essential. You can also use two ties in the trailer, in case one breaks.

Trailer Ties

A trailer tie should be strong, and it should be long enough so that your horse can move back against the rump chain without feeling pressure on his head. It should be securely attached to a ring or mount in the trailer. It should be able to be released quickly.

This gives you a lot of choices. You can use your regular lead rope — a round cotton or poly rope is best — tied in a quick-release knot.

You can also use a special trailer tie — usually no longer than twenty-four inches long — that remains permanently in your trailer. The trailer tie should have at least one panic snap. Better ties have two panic snaps, one at each end.

The ultimate in trailer tie safety is a stretchy tie with two panic snaps. The stretchiness helps calm your horse by making him feel less restrained if he pulls back, and the double snaps ensure that you can let him loose quickly.

For young or small horses or ponies, you can use a bale of hay tied securely to the rump chain. If the horse pulls back he comes against the familiar — and prickly — bale. He is calmed by feeling a boundary behind him. The greater the distance between the horse's rump and the rump chain, the more helpful adding the hay bale becomes. Don't scrunch the horse forward though. He should have plenty of room to shift and balance himself.

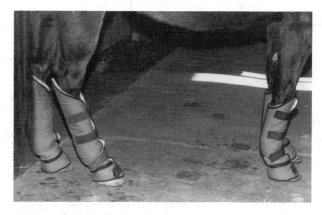

These shipping boots fasten with velcro and protect both the legs and hooves.

A head bumper buckles to your horse's halter and prevents your horse from injuring his poll (the highest point on his body) in a trailer.

Loading

The first rule in loading your horse into a van or trailer is to go slowly. Leave yourself plenty of time. If you are late already, forget about your morning classes, and aim to get to the show in time for lunch. Giving your horse a pleasant loading experience is much more important than any horse show ribbon.

Park the trailer where there is plenty of room around it. If your horse objects to loading, you don't want him to trample flowerbeds or back into fences.

Pull on the truck's emergency brake. Have someone at the escape door ready to open it once your horse is secured inside. You want to be able to get out, but you don't want your horse to assume that door is for him to escape through.

Hang up a net filled with hay where your horse will be able to reach it once he is loaded.

If your trailer has a ramp, make sure it is solidly placed so it doesn't wobble. If the ground is uneven, find some solid blocks to place under the ramp so it remains steady.

Maybe your horse loads easily. You can just lead him confidently into the trailer. Have your helper snap the rump chain behind him, and close the tailgate. Then tie your horse. Make sure the tie is long enough so that your horse feels the restraints behind him before the halter rope tightens.

Maybe your horse doesn't load this easily. Many good horses don't — and from their point of view, it makes sense to be hesitant. They're about to be confined in a small, dark space for an unknown length of time. When

---

TRAVELING IN SEVERE HEAT

Hauling in severe heat and humidity brings its own concerns. Horses aren't really built to handle tropical-type heat, and traveling in a horse van or trailer makes the heat very difficult to avoid.

Take these precautions.

- Travel at night, if possible. It may disrupt your sleep schedule, but it will spare your horse a lot of stress.
- Keep your trailer as open as possible. All windows should be open, and you should take off the back door curtains for maximum airflow.
- Never leave your horse in a parked trailer in the sun. If you must park and can't find shade, take the horse out of the trailer.
- For extra cooling, bed your trailer extra-deep in shavings, and then wet them with cool water. Or get blocks of ice and secure them in the front of the trailer, where the breeze will blow across them onto your horse.

---

they get out again they'll be a long way from home. I wouldn't go into a trailer either, if that was all I knew about it!

Be patient. If the horse pauses at the entrance of the trailer, give him a moment to let his eyes adjust.

Moving the center divider over to create a wider entry way often helps. Make sure you secure the divider so it won't swing back as you are loading.

If the horse sees you walk in ahead of him it often helps. Picking up one front foot at a time and placing them on the ramp sometimes works to instill confidence.

Ask your horse for one step at a time, and thank him with a scratch on the neck or a handful of grain when he takes that step.

If your horse still strongly and violently resists loading, you need expert help. The combination of a rebellious horse and a small, confined space is a recipe for trouble. Don't attempt to train your horse to load by yourself. One or both of you could get hurt. And if you fail, you'll reinforce your horse's belief that he doesn't have to go inside that thing.

Ask your instructor to recommend a good trainer who will teach your horse to load calmly and confidently.

At the Show

IN THIS SECTION

Safe showing involves:
- ✔ Giving your horse time to relax
- ✔ Watching out for others
- ✔ Following show rules

Once you've gotten to the show, you can take steps to make sure this is a safe, confidence-building experience for both you and your horse.

■ **Give your horse plenty of time to get used to new surroundings.** Arrive early. Lead him around the show grounds. Try to anticipate which things might frighten him later, and give him a chance to inspect them now, while there's no pressure. Strange horse trailers, piles of equipment, the judge's stand or tent, refreshment areas, are all good things to check out. (This long, slow walk will give <u>you</u> a chance to calm down, too.)

■ **Tie your horse safely or not at all.** At many competitions, where you'll only be on the grounds for the day, there will be no stabling available. People usually tie their horses to the sides of the trailers. This can be dangerous. Your trailer is just a big metal box. If it's an older model, many of its edges will be sharp and unprotected. The edges on newer models should be covered with protective rubber. This rubber can wear off or even be torn off, and even covered edges can be sharp.

If you must tie your horse to the trailer, make sure all edges — including the lower edge of the trailer body — are protected, and don't leave the horse unattended.

Using an elastic tie like a bungee cord or The Leader is a good idea, and can save your trailer from being pulled apart if your horse starts suddenly.

Don't tie your horse where he's apt to be frightened by other vehicles pulling alongside. Don't tie him where he can kick other trailers or horses or where there's a lot of pedestrian traffic. And don't leave him alone. Try to have someone else along with you at the show who can watch your horse if you need to be away, or who can lead him around.

■ **Expect your horse to behave differently at shows, especially at first.** Unless he has been shown frequently, showing is a strange and exciting event for him. He's going to be nervous, and that means he won't be listening to you as carefully as he normally does. He may be harder to stop or turn. Bad habits that you thought you'd conquered may suddenly reappear. Things he's normally not bothered by, like fly spray or hosing, may suddenly be a big deal. It's best to have a reliable system for redirecting his attention, such as a bucket of treats. This will help keep him focused and easier to handle.

Be patient about this. It isn't fair to punish a horse who's excited by a new situation. Just persist quietly in what you need to do. Your quietness will have a good influence on your horse.

Follow the Rules

When you and your horse are away from home, follow the rules of the show or clinic.

■ **Clean up manure and bedding.**

■ **Be courteous, and think of others.** Let other riders know if you are about to pass in the ring. If you're passing from opposite directions, go right shoulder to right shoulder. Remember to keep a safe distance between horses. Keep your eyes open for possible traffic jams in the showring, and be prepared to circle back or cross to the other side of the ring.

Rules for shows are different in different parts of the country. Ask your instructor to review them with you at least a week before the show and keep them in mind as you practice.

- **Watch out for people on foot.** Don't be one of those riders who come close to running down the judge or the ringmaster. Keep your eyes open.

- **Don't share equipment with others, especially buckets and bits.** Diseases are often transmitted at shows, as strange horses come in contact with one another. Try to limit that contact, either direct or indirect.

LOW-KEY EVENTS TO HELP YOU GET STARTED

Schooling competitions offer low-key experience with an emphasis on learning.

When you start taking your horse to competitions, it's best to start slowly. Both you and your horse will be more relaxed if you treat your first few shows as schooling opportunities. Ask your instructor to attend a small, low-key, local event or open show with you. The experience will help you get used to the routine.

If you belong to the Pony Club or 4-H, camps are a good way to take your horse into a show-like atmosphere. You'll be there long enough for your horse — and you — to get thoroughly relaxed. You'll have lessons in riding and handling, you'll introduce your horse to new surroundings, and you'll have a chance to make new friends.

You can also try a one- or two-day clinic in the kind of riding or driving you want to pursue. This gives your horse exposure to other horses and strange surroundings, with lots of supervision.

Once you're ready to compete, check out local horse shows. Ask around. And remember, local doesn't always mean small. Find out what the show atmosphere is like.

If you are a trail rider, look for a short, friendly ride nearby. You may be able to find rides that are not competitive, which will reduce the pressures on you and your horse.

If you're interested in dressage, three-day horse trials, or hunting and jumping, look for a schooling show. The atmosphere will be quiet and friendly, and the emphasis will be on learning.

Small gymkhanas, where you'll play games on horseback, can be a fun, confidence-boosting experience.

In the West, you might look for small open shows that have both English and Western categories.

Remember Your Limitations

Try to remember who you are, and who your horse is. Just because the two of you are excited doesn't mean you can suddenly jump six feet or turn on a dime. The hardest and most important thing in any competition is to remember your limitations. And that's up to you. Your horse can't do it. He's capable of ignoring a lot of physical pain and danger when he's excited. It's your responsibility to keep him from hurting himself. If you're in a jump-off and the fences go too high for him, it's sensible and honorable to pull out. If you're trail riding and he seems overheated or lame, quit. A good horseman always thinks of the horse first, before any ribbon or trophy. Other good horsemen will respect you for your decision.

Think of Other Riders

There will be a lot of people at any competition who aren't following these rules, or any rules. They don't know how to ride well, they care more about winning than about the well-being of their horses — they had bad luck, fell off, broke a piece of equipment. You could suddenly see an out-of-control or riderless horse galloping toward you. You may find people riding up close on your horse's heels, cutting you off at corners, spooking a horse up while you're trying to calm yours down.

Try to be alert to what's going on around you. Watch out for other horses and riders, but watch out for pedestrians, too. Many spectators don't know how to behave around horses. They may come up behind your horse unexpectedly, try to feed him treats or pat him — little kids and dogs may even walk underneath him. Don't be afraid to tell these strangers what to do or not to do. Their own safety as well as yours may depend on it.

Have Fun!

Horse shows are hard, but they aren't a matter of life or death. Have fun! That's what you're here for — to show off your lovely horse, to learn, to play, to find out if you're as good as you think you are. Relax. Make it an enjoyable day. You and your horse will both get more out of it that way.

FINAL THOUGHTS

You've learned a lot of rules about housing, handling, and riding your horse. These rules will help keep you safer, and ensure that the partnership between you and your horse is happy and productive.

But rules alone aren't enough. They help you get started being a safe and considerate horse owner. But the unexpected *will* happen. You will undoubtedly meet with situations that aren't described in this book; horses that react in unusual ways; instructors who have different ideas and different ways of doing things.

Your thinking should be based on an ever-increasing knowledge of horses. You should be guided by the goal of keeping your horse relaxed and allowing her time to learn. You should always reject suggestions based on inflicting fear or pain, which can only have a negative long-term effect.

If you don't know what to do about a problem you're having with your horse, don't be afraid to ask a professional. All horsemen need to learn from one another — even the best. And don't be ashamed to send your horse back to a trainer if you think that's what she needs.

The quicker you seek profesional help, the cheaper, quicker, and easier it will be to solve the problem. If you wait and try to solve the problem yourself or receive bad advice about it, the problem can become bigger and more dangerous. A well-qualified trainer may be able to fix a big problem, but by then the horse has learned to push the limits and is not necessarily safe for the novice rider.

So think ahead and plan for the long term. Doing so will extend your horse's years of health and usefulness, and will give you many more years of riding fun.

BUYING A SAFE HORSE

Buying a horse is always chancy, but there are some rules to follow that will help ensure that the horse you get is safe, sound, good–natured, and well trained.

To Locate a Good Horse for Sale:

■ **Ask the leader of your local Pony Club branch or 4-H horse–manship group.** She may know of a horse that a group member has outgrown. This is the ideal solution — a well-known, well-trained animal who's used to taking care of a novice rider.

■ **Ask an experienced and respected instructor or trainer for the names of reputable local horse-dealers.** Go to a dealer who has been established in your area for some time, and who expects to stay around for some time to come. People like this usually make a special effort to match a horse to a rider, to be honest, and to be sure their customers are satisfied.

■ **Horse breeders are another good potential source.** They, too, tend to be people with reputations to maintain. You'll also have the chance to see what your horse's sire and dam are like.

■ *Never* **buy a horse at an auction,** unless you are a very experienced person with a lot of time and money to throw away. It is practically impossible to learn anything about a horse's background or history at an auction. His health is always suspect. There are all kinds of ways of temporarily improving even severe health conditions in order to make a quick sale.

Buying Checklist

Here is a list of precautions you should take when going out to buy a horse.

✔ **Don't buy a stallion,** even if he appears to be very gentle and well trained. Stallions are for experienced horsemen *only*.

✔ **Don't buy an unbroken youngster,** unless you are fully prepared to have it trained professionally, and to wait until your young horse is a safe mount. Don't buy a young horse and expect to learn together. One of you needs to be experienced in order for your partnership to prosper.

✔ **Have your instructor or an experienced horseman come with you** — someone who knows your abilities and what you hope to do with the horse. Your riding teacher would be an ideal choice.

✔ **If possible, see the horse in a setting close to what your own facility will provide** — that is, stalled or in a pasture. A horse used to such conditions will adjust to his new home more easily.

✔ **Ask how long the current seller has had the horse,** who his previous owner was, and what kind of conditions that owner provided.

✔ **Watch the horse while he is loose in stall or pasture.** Note his attitude as you and the owner approach. If he's not eating, he should appear friendly and interested. If he comes toward you with his ears forward, that's a very good sign. Note if he's easy to catch and halter. Note his expression as the halter is put on. Does he pull away or seem headshy?

✔ **Have the horse tied as you will be tying him at home** — either at cross-ties or single hitch. Let him stand for half an hour while you talk over his history with the seller. Watch for signs of impatience — pulling back, stamping, or pawing.

✔ **Groom him, or watch the owner groom him.** Observe carefully to see if anything makes him wince. Watch how he reacts to being bathed and having fly spray put on. Note how he behaves as his feet are handled. He should allow them to be held up for as long as necessary without pulling or threatening to kick.

✔ **Watch as the owner leads him around for you.** As well as his gaits — and signs of lameness — you are looking for manners. Does he respect the leader's personal space? Is he easy to stop and turn? Does the owner seem easy and confident about handling this horse, or does he take precautions such as putting the chain shank over his nose or under his chin? Does the horse nip as he is led?

✔ **Observe as the horse is saddled and bridled.** Does he wince or nip as the girth is tightened? This may indicate a sore back. Does he bloat? (That's no reason not to buy him, but it will be useful knowledge to have.) Does he take the bit willingly? Does he object to having his ears handled?

✔ **Note what kind of bit the horse is being worked with.** For a horse being ridden English, it should be a mild, thick snaffle, or perhaps a Pelham. For a Western horse, it should be a mild, low-port curb. Any thing extreme, such as a twisted snaffle or a high-port curb, should set off warning bells in your mind.

✔ **Ask the seller to ride the horse before you do.** The seller should be willing to do this. Any reluctance is a warning sign.

✔ **Ask to see all three gaits demonstrated.** Watch the transitions between gaits closely. This is where poor training will show up. Does the horse seem difficult to stop or slow down? Is the rider pulling hard on the reins, causing him to open his mouth? Does he throw his head up in the air, or shake it? These may be bad signs — or they may simply show that the seller is a poor rider. You'll be better able to tell when you ride him yourself, and when your expert adviser does.

✔ **Ask to see all three gaits performed both at large — all the way around the rail of the ring — and in smaller circles.** Ask to see the horse go in both directions. Does he tend to gather speed uncontrollably at trot or canter? If the owner will only canter him a very short distance, this may be a sign that he tends to get out of control. Does he tend to slow down frequently? Is the rider always kicking to keep him going? This may be a sign of laziness, or unsoundness. Does he handle equally well in both directions? Most horses and riders have one preferred direction of travel (clockwise or counterclockwise) and may seem slightly rough or awkward going the other way. Some degree of this is to be expected. But anything extreme may be a sign of bad training or unsoundness.

After the seller has demonstrated the horse, it's time for you and your instructor to try him out.

✔ **Feed and tack him up yourself.** Ride him, following the same rules you asked the seller to follow — all three gaits, both directions. Expect the horse to feel strange to you. Horses' gaits and body movements can differ widely, and it will take you a while to get used to a new mount.

✔ **Look for things that may continue to make you uncomfortable** — jarring gaits, difficulty in stopping the horse, a tendency to get out of control at the canter. Your instructor should be able to discuss these concerns with you, and tell you which problems you'll be able to over come with better training for either you or the horse.

✔ **Ask:**

> How old is the horse?
> Where does he come from? (Name of breeder, if possible)
> Who trained him?
> What kind of work has he done?
> Does he stand tied?
> Is he good in traffic?
> Has he ever been lame? Seriously ill?
> Does he load easily into a trailer?
> Is he easy to shoe and trim?
> Any problems with bridling?
> Any saddling problems? History of a sore back?
> Names of previous owners?
> Names of vet and farrier who have cared for him?

✔ **Don't buy a horse after only one look.** If you like him very much, have him vetted. Bring your own veterinarian along to check the horse out thoroughly, or haul the horse to a vet.

✔ **Ask for a trial period.** Be aware that not all dealers or breeders will be willing to turn a horse over to an individual and you may have to board with a professional for a week or two. The added expense will be well worth it whether you keep the horse or not.

In Sum

You can take every precaution described above and still end up with a bad horse. However, if you follow the guidelines you will have substantially improved your chances of getting a good horse. The most important thing to do is admit your own limitations, and ask for advice. No one will think less of you for doing so. Benefit as much as you can from the knowledge of those around you. Talking horse is one of the great pleasures in life, and most horsemen are happy for an excuse.

Appendix B

SOURCES

Equipment

Biothane Tack

Parry Harness & Tack
Foster Road, Verona, NY 13478
315-363-6173
Parry is a good source for light-weight, durable synthetic tack.

Fencing

The Colorado Kiwi Company
Box 7738386, West Hwy. 40
Steamboat Springs, CO 80477
303-879-3823

NASCO Farm & Ranch Catalog
901 Janesville Avenue, Fort Atkinson, WI
53538-0901
414-563-2446
NASCO is a good source of fencing and farm supplies.

Premier
P.O. Box 895, Washington, IA 52353
800-282-6631
Premier offers many innovative electric fence systems, as well as hi-tensile. They publish an informative Fencing Guide.

Springfield Fence Co. Inc.
359 River St., P.O. Box 517, Springfield,
VT 05156
802-886-2221

Fire Protection

Stock Safe Fire Protection Systems
103 Powwow River Road, East Kingston,
NH 03827
603-642-9998 or 800-551-1988

Foot Free Safety Stirrup

Equestrian International Products
71 Ore Hill, South Kent, CT 06785
203-927-3292
Has introduced the Foot Free Safety Stirrups to the U.S.

General

The Australian Connection
Janet Pucci and Joan Dowis
9274 Muir Way, Granite Bay, CA 95746
916-791-1542
A good source of equipment for the endurance rider.

Dover Saddlery
Box 5837, Holliston, MA 01746
1-800-989-1500
A complete supply of tack, clothing, and supplies for English riders.

High Brook Horse & Harness
(A Miller dealer)
Route 106, P.O. Box 325, South
Woodstock, VT 05071
802-457-4677
Miller's is one of the foremost tack dealers in the U.S., with a complete line of high quality gear for English riders. High Brook stocks Miller's equipment and also handles mail orders.

Kentucky Tack Shop
3380 Paris Pike, Lexington, KY 40511
606-293-1696

The Maryland Saddlery
Mail Order Division
15005 Falls Road, Butler, MD 21023
410-472-3114
Puts out a catalogue just for kids, with a good selection of child-sized gear and helmets.

Miller Harness Co., Inc.
235 Murray Hill Parkway, East
Rutherford, NJ 07073
(See note under High Brook)

Smucker's Harness Shop, Inc.
2014 Main Street (Churchtown), Narvon,
PA 17555
215-445-5956
Smucker's is a great source for all types of harness, as well as English and Western tack and supplies.

State Line Tack, Inc.
Route 121, P.O. Box 428, Plaistow, NH
03865
800-228-9208
State Line publishes catalogues for English and Western riding. Prices are usually among the lowest available.

Helmets

Equine Science Marketing Pty. Ltd.
8A Adina Court, Tullamarine 3043,
Australia
61-3-330-3448

International Riding Helmets, Inc.
205 Industrial Loop, Staten Island, NY
10309
718-356-1640

Lexington Safety Products
480 Fairman Road, Lexington, KY 40511
606-233-1404

North American Riding for the Handicapped Association (NARHA)
P.O. Box 33150, Denver, CO 80233
800-369-RIDE

Troxel Cycling and Fitness
1333 30th Street, San Diego, CA 92154
619-429-1441

Stable Equipment

California Carriage & Harness Company
24030 Frampton Avenue, Harbor City, CA 90710
1-800-635-6289

Country Manufacturing, Inc.
333 Salem Avenue Extension
P.O. Box 104, Fredericktown, OH 43019
614-694-9926
    A source for stall modules and estate equipment such as manure spreaders and wagons. Also carry the Thermo-Bucket.

Equuspring Horse Waterer
1436 West Reindeer Road, Lancaster, TX 75146-4733
214-227-8093
    Good source of safe waterers.

Tail Lights, Saddles

Marciante Saddle & Leather Co., Inc.
214 Thompson Avenue, Glendale, CA 91201
818-247-0434
    A source for Tail Lights, which can make you safer when riding at dusk.

Western Safety Helmets

American Riding Instructor Certification Program
P.O. Box 282, Alton Bay, NH 03810
603-875-40000

Horsemanship Safety Association
Drawer 39, Fentress, TX 78622
512-488-2220

Organizations and Associations

American Association of Horsemanship Safety
Drawer 39, Fentress, TX 78622
512-488-2220**American Medical**

American Medical Equestrian Association
103 Surrey Road, Waynesville, NC 28786
704-456-3392

American Riding Instructor Certification Program
P.O. Box 282, Alton Bay, NH 03810
603-875-4000

Horsemanship Safety Association
517 Bear Road
Lake Placid, FL 33852
800-798-8106

North American Riding for the Handicapped Association
(NARHA)
P.O. Box 33150, Denver, CO 80233
800-369-RIDE

Safety Equipment Institute
1901 North Moore Street, Arlington, VA 22209
703-525-1695

U.S. Pony Clubs, Inc.
The Kentucky Horse Park.
4071 Iron Works Pike, Lexington, KY 40511
606-254-7669

Bibliography

Denby-Wrightson, Kathryn, and Fry, Joan. *The Beginning Dressage Book.* New York, NY: Arco, 1981.

Fisk, Jeanna C. *How Horses Learn*, Brattleboro, VT: Stephen Green Press. 1982.

Hill, Cherry. *Horsekeeping On a Small Acreage.* Pownal, VT: Garden Way Publishing, Inc., 1990.

Mettler, John J., Jr., DVM. *Horse Sense.* Pownal, VT: Garden Way Publishing, Inc., 1989.

Richardson, Julie, ed. *Horse Tack.* New York, NY: Morrow, 1981.

Schäfer, Michael. *The Language of the Horse.* New York, NY: Kaye & Ward/Arco, 1975.

Straiton, E.C. *The Horse Owner's Vet Book.* Philadelphia, PA: J.B. Lippincott Company, 1973.

Swift, Sally. *Centered Riding.* North Pomfret, NY: Trafalgar Square/St. Martin's, 1985.

Tellington-Jones, Linda. *The Tellington-Jones Equine Awareness Method.* Millwood, CO: Breakthrough, 1985.

Young, John Richard. *Schooling For Young Riders.* Norman, OK: University of Oklahoma Press, 1970.

INDEX

Page references in *italics* indicate photographs and line drawings.